Madame Maigret's Recipes

Madame

With a Letter-Preface by

Georges Simenon

Translated from the French by

Mary Manheim

Drawings by

Nikolaus E. Wolff

Wine Glossary by

Jack Lang

A Helen and Kurt Wolff Book

Harcourt Brace Jovanovich

Maigret's Recipes

Presented by

Robert J. Courtine

New York and London

Printed in the United States of America

Library of Congress Cataloging in Publication Data

Courtine, Robert J
    Madame Maigret's recipes.

    "A Helen and Kurt Wolff book."
    Includes index.
    1. Cookery, French.   I. Title.
TX719.C6117713   641.5′944   75-6540
ISBN 0-15-154990-7

First edition
B C D E

This cookbook was compiled by
Robert Courtine on the occasion of
Georges Simenon's seventieth birthday.

Letter–Preface

My dear Courtine,

A good many years ago I resolved not to write any more prefaces; they demanded too much of the time needed for my novels and their number diluted their value. May I therefore beg you to consider as a preface this letter written with all the sincerity of a friend.

I have been reading and admiring you over a long period of time. Gastronomy has become a prevalent hobby, particularly in recent years, and there is hardly a newspaper or magazine without its food column. But mostly the cooking described there is of a fancifulness that goes better with inflatable plastic furniture than with the solid comfort of a dining room.

I am tempted to call you the last surviving classic, but this might scare away all those who prize originality above all. For every dish, you have painstakingly traced its origins, more often than not to peasant sources; you have searched for the reason for its cooking method, its trimmings, and such and such ingredient. And frequently you have arrived at simplified versions adapted to the enfeebled stomachs of the present.

I have watched you at work. Your curiosity and your diligence never cease to amaze me. And whenever I am faced with a matter of ambiguity, it is to you that I turn for advice.

Your old friend Cornovsky has been labeled "Prince of Gastronomers." You deserve to inherit this title, though I find it somewhat pompous and would prefer the term "expert."

Experts are those who can distinguish between fake and genuine paintings, between tawdry art works and the real thing. This is what you do for cooking, which is also an art, and perhaps the most ancient.

You know of my admiration. By way of this letter-preface, I hope to extend it to those rare readers who as yet are not aware of who you are.

Yours in friendship, my dear Courtine,

Georges Simenon

Foreword

Holding his jacket over one arm, Maigret put his key in
the lock. He called out his traditional "It's me!" and
sniffed, trying to guess from the smell what there would
be for lunch. . . .

L'Amoureux de Madame Maigret

In Paris, on Boulevard Richard-Lenoir, if spring had
at last reached there too, Madame Maigret would
certainly have opened the windows and tidied the room,
in dressing gown and slippers, while a stew would be
simmering on the stove.

Maigret Afraid

When Louise was a young girl in Colmar, her parents were determined
to find her a husband in the Highway Department.

Madame Maigret's family—the Schoellers, Kurts, and Léonards—
had always been connected with that respected branch of the civil
service. But in all Alsace, from Strasbourg to Colmar to Mulhouse,
there wasn't an acceptable suitor to be found, and in the end they sent
her to Paris to stay with her uncle and aunt Léonard, trusting—and
that was their only reason for sending her—that they would find her a
husband.

By some quirk of fate young Jules Maigret, who had just doffed
the uniform of a traffic cop and become the secretary of a *commissaire*,
turned up at the Léonards' one evening and won her heart. She was a
trifle on the plump side at the time, with a fresh country complexion
and a sparkle in her eyes that was all her own. The famous *commissaire*
tells the whole story in his *Memoirs*.

He was so bashful that she almost had to force his hand before he
finally proposed to her. Besides being bashful, he realized that the
police is not the Highway Department.

During that first evening at the Léonards—an old school friend had
brought him—Louise, the "girl in the blue dress," had hardly spoken
to him. She had merely called his attention to some little cakes with

little pieces of candied fruit on them, and said: "They've left the best ones. Try these."

These words were spoken with a look of complicity that delights me as it must have delighted the future *commissaire*, because it was the beginning of a culinary relationship inseparable from their love.

And indeed, if Simenon is at such pains to establish the image of a "good housewife," always at her stove, always scrubbing and polishing, always coddling her big baby of a husband, it is because that is the very essence of their married life. Like Catherine in the Alsatian song, Louise knows how to make

> A cherry tart
> To win your heart . . .

She reminds me of the lines written by that great gourmand, Théodore de Banville, in praise of his wife:

> While pallid Phyllis, to preserve her band-
> Box beauty hardly dares to lift a hand
> But languishes from couch to chair to bed,
> You wash the clothes and cook and bake the bread.
> Your touch is light, yet firm. You even know
> How to make patties wrapped in flaky dough.

Like the good, honest woman she is, Louise Maigret goes in for good honest cookery that hits the spot with Maigret. Sophisticated cuisine has no appeal for him. On one occasion he had dinner at the house of a childhood friend who had grown rich and pretentious: "Of course, the dinner was excellent, but he had no taste for these complicated dishes, these sauces invariably studded with truffles or crayfish tails. . . ."

Cooking comes as naturally to Louise Maigret as song to a bird. When the *commissaire* tells her about some succulent dish he has eaten away from home—for people will talk of what they have had to eat— she makes a note of it: she'll track the recipe down and surprise him with it someday.

She exchanges recipes with her friend, Dr. Pardon's wife (at whose home the Maigrets dine once a month, returning their hospitality two weeks later).

These recipes are added to her ancestral repertory, which came from Alsace like the Schoellers and the Kurts. And like the *prunelle* that her married sister brings her when she comes to Paris.

She copies her recipes carefully in an old notebook that Maigret brought home one day when he'd gone to a stationery store in lower Montmartre in search of information. This was one of his first cases. He had bought two enormous notebooks with red covers to appease the ill-tempered old woman who kept the store. In the other notebook, Madame Maigret has pasted newspaper articles about the *commissaire*, which she still clips religiously.

Of course, this second notebook is her favorite.

But we, who are familiar with all Maigret's cases, are delighted to have been entrusted, thanks to the kindness of Georges Simenon (for whom Louise Maigret has an unmistakable weakness), with the precious book of recipes: the recipes of Madame Maigret!

Robert J. Courtine

Contents

Shellfish

Fish

Variety Meats— Tripe, Calf's Head, Kidney, Liver, etc.

Meat

Some Vegetables, a Dish of Mushrooms, and a Bowl of Spaghetti

Desserts

Soups

Soupe aux Tomates

(*Tomato Soup*)

First they served tomato soup along with a Saint-Émilion so sweet it turned your stomach. It had obviously been doctored for export.

A Crime in Holland

"What kind of soup do you have?" he called out, sitting down on a crate.
"Tomato."
"Fine."

Maigret Returns

- Peel and mince a large onion and a small clove of garlic.
- Cut 7 large ripe tomatoes into quarters and scoop out the seeds.
- Fry onion, garlic, and tomatoes in goose fat. Place in a large saucepan.
- Add 4⅓ cups of chicken stock (or bouillon). Salt and pepper to taste.
- When tomatoes are thoroughly cooked, strain the soup, pushing the tomatoes through strainer with the back of a spoon. Put strained soup back in the saucepan.
- Add 2 Tb. of very fine vermicelli noodles and cook briefly. (The noodles should be firm, not soft and mushy.)
- Brown slices (one per person) of whole-grain bread in butter.
- Place a slice of bread in each soup bowl.
- Pour the soup over the bread and sprinkle with freshly cut chervil. Serve.

COURTINE'S NOTE: This soup is good only when made with garden-fresh tomatoes. The chervil (and all fresh herbs) should be cut with scissors and not chopped with a knife, in order to preserve their flavor.

With the tomato soup, Maigret drank *Quincy*.

Soupe à l'Oignon Gratinée

(*Onion Soup Gratinéed with Cheese*)

The two men had barely finished their *soupe à l'oignon gratinée* when the waiter set down before them lavish servings of *choucroutes garnies* and two more pints of beer.

To Any Length

Neither one was hungry, nevertheless they sat down at a table in a brasserie and, because they had decided to an hour before, ordered *soupe à l'oignon gratinée*.

Maigret and the Young Girl

- Cook 1 lb. of thinly sliced onions in some lard. Sprinkle them with 2 Tb. of flour. Turn the floured onions with a wooden spatula until they are brown.
- Add about 6 cups of beef stock (or bouillon) and salt and pepper to taste. Simmer for 30 minutes.
- Strain the soup.
- Brown several slices of stale French bread in butter.
- Put 3 Tb. of Madeira in a deep ovenproof dish. Add a layer of browned bread slices, a layer of grated Swiss Gruyère cheese, a layer of bread slices, terminating with a layer of cheese.
- Beat 2 whole eggs with 1 tsp. Madeira and stir it into the soup.
- Pour the soup into the dish containing the bread and cheese and bake until the cheese is golden brown.

COURTINE'S NOTE: It is important to use real Swiss Gruyère cheese in this recipe.

With the *gratinée*, Maigret had light beer.

Vichyssoise

They ended up by ordering some cool, refreshing
Vichyssoise, followed by *canard à l'orange*—the
specialty of the day.

Maigret on the Defensive

- Wash, peel, and finely chop leeks (3 cups). Sauté them in butter until they are soft but not colored.
- Peel and quarter 4 medium-sized potatoes and place in the pan with the leeks. Add the neck, wings, and feet of a chicken and 4½ cups of water. Salt. Cover and simmer for ½ hour.
- Remove the chicken parts and put the soup through a vegetable mill or blender, then strain it through a piece of cheesecloth. Let the soup cool, stirring it from time to time. Cover with a piece of buttered paper and place in the refrigerator.
- When the soup is ice-cold, stir in 2 cups of heavy cream. Taste for salt. Add a dash of cayenne pepper.
- Pour into soup cups.
- Sprinkle the soup in the cups with finely cut fresh chives.

COURTINE'S NOTE: It is important to use *boiling* potatoes (the kind that disintegrate while cooking) in this dish. .

With the Vichyssoise, Maigret drank *Saint-Pourçain blanc*.

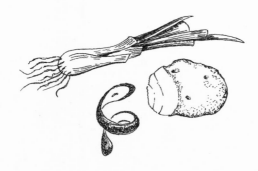

Sauces

Mayonnaise

"It's me" he said, coming in the hallway which smelled
strongly of grilled blood sausage. And holding the lobster
behind his back: "Tell me, Felicie . . . Do you know
how to make mayonnaise at least?"

A haughty smile.

"Good! Then you can start making some as soon as
you've put this fellow on to cook."

Félicie est là

Here as well, the window was wide open. For dinner,
just as during the finest days of summer, there were
cold meats, salad, and mayonnaise.

Maigret and the Madwoman

"As for you—I know you're going to have some *andouillette*. . . . And I'm going to treat myself to some cold
lobster with mayonnaise."

Maigret et le Fantôme

Mayonnaise for Cold Meats:
- Place 3 egg yolks, ¼ tsp. salt, 6 Tb. vinegar, and 1½ tsp. strong
  prepared mustard in a bowl. Beat rapidly with a wire whisk.
- Starting with drops and increasing to teaspoons then to tablespoons,
  add 2 cups of pure olive oil. Each drop or spoonful of oil should
  be well beaten in before the next is added.
- When all the oil has been added, beat in rapidly 1–2 Tb. of
  boiling-hot vinegar. Taste for salt.*

* This can all be done in a blender.

Mayonnaise for Lobster:
- Use the recipe above but substitute peanut oil for olive oil and use a very strong prepared mustard (½ tsp. rather than 1½ tsp.).
- Whip ⅓ cup of cream.
- Mix the juice of ½ lemon with ½ tsp. of strong mustard (mentioned above), and add to the cream. Then add the cream to the mayonnaise.
- Taste for salt. Add a pinch of cayenne pepper. Beat rapidly with a wire whisk and serve.

COURTINE'S NOTE: There's only one "trick" to making mayonnaise. Be sure your eggs and oil are the same (fairly low) temperature.

Entrées

Filets de Harengs

(Herring Fillets)

"Bring us a carafe of *Beaujolais* right away. What's
on the menu?"

"*Andouillettes*. Just came in from Auvergne this
morning."

Maigret decided to start with *filets de harengs*.

Maigret and the Madwoman

- Purchase 1 lb. of fillets of salt herring. Wash them in milk and let
  them soak in the same milk for 48 hours. Drain. Place them on
  paper toweling to dry.
- In an oval earthenware dish, place a layer of carrots cut in rounds.
  Place a thick layer of herring fillets on top of the carrots along with
  a few peppercorns and a few whole cloves. Add another layer of
  carrots and sliced onions. Add a layer of herring and finally a layer
  of thinly sliced onions. Add enough olive oil to cover. Place wax
  paper over the dish and set in a cool place for 48 hours.
- Cook good-quality boiling potatoes in their jackets. Drain them and
  place them in a hot oven for several minutes to dry. Serve with the
  herring.

COURTINE'S NOTE: Slightly toasted whole-grain bread should be
served with this dish along with salt butter, for herring prepared
this way should not be salty.

With the *filets de harengs*, Maigret drank *Beaujolais primeur*.

Pâté de Campagne

"Can we eat here?"

"Of course . . . What would you like? Veal roast with sorrel? Roast pork with lentils? . . . We have a good *pâté de campagne* as a starter."

The Most Obstinate Man in Paris

- Remove the skin and membranes (or ask your butcher to do this) from a medium-sized pork liver. Put it through a meat grinder using the finest blade so as to obtain a thick purée.
- Chop 1 lb. of lean fresh pork and the same amount of fresh fat back (*lard gras*). (If you cannot find fat back, substitute fat salt pork, first simmering it for 10 minutes in water to remove salt—Tr.)
- Mix these ingredients thoroughly in a bowl, add 1 peeled clove of garlic, 3 peeled and minced shallots, 2 tsp. of salt, ½ tsp. of pepper, and a pinch of allspice.
- Spread a large piece of caul fat* (*crépine*) previously soaked in lukewarm water, then wiped dry, on the table.
- Place the contents of the bowl in the middle of the caul fat. Pick up the edges of the fat and fold and mold them around the meat mixture until the finished product has the form of a football.
- Place 5 or 6 thin strips of pork rind (not smoked) in a heavy pan and set the ball-shaped meat mixture in the middle. Around this arrange a cracked veal bone, some pork bones, a sliced onion, a carrot cut in rounds, and a *bouquet garni*. Add ½ cup of dry white wine and 1 Tb. of *prunelle* (plum brandy). Cover and place in a slow oven (about 300°) for 2½ hours. When done it should be a rich golden brown.
- Baste the pâté from time to time with the juices formed in cooking.
- Carefully remove the pâté from the pan. Drain it and pack it into a round earthenware baking dish.
- Melt some lard and pour it over the lukewarm pâté so as to cover it with a layer of fat approximately ¾ inch in thickness. When the pâté has completely cooled, place it in the refrigerator.

* Caul fat—the lacy membrane that lines the visceral cavity of a hog. It can be procured in America, though you may have to order it.   Tr.

COURTINE'S NOTE: The pâté will keep as is for several days in the refrigerator. Should you wish to keep it longer, cover with a sheet of clear plastic wrap, letting the plastic hang down well over the edges of the dish, and place over this a tight-fitting cover.

TRANSLATOR'S NOTE: A *bouquet garni* is a combination of parsley, thyme, and bay leaf (either fresh or dried). The best method is to tie these loosely in a piece of cheesecloth (wash it out first) so they can be removed easily before the dish is served. A normal *bouquet garni* is composed of 2 sprigs of parsley, ½ bay leaf, and a sprig (or ¼ tsp.) of thyme. Hereafter in this book, any mention of a *bouquet garni* will be referred back to this note unless there is something special about it. In that case, the ingredients will be given.

With the *pâté de campagne*, Maigret drank *Cornas*.

Andouillettes*

He ate his roast beef without much appetite. His wife was wondering why, when all of a sudden he said: "Tomorrow you'll make us some *andouillettes*. . . ."
Maigret and the Saturday Caller

They served *andouillettes* with French fried potatoes. . . . Maigret filled the glasses.
Maigrét et le Fantôme

"What is there for lunch?"

"*Andouillette* . . . But if you'd rather have steak . . ."
Maigret and the Informer

"How's the food at the *Petit Saint Paul?*"

"The boss does the cooking, and if you like *andouillettes*, hers are the best in the whole neighborhood."
Maigret and the Lazy Burglar

- Choose *andouillettes* made in the traditional manner of uncut chitterlings.
- The *andouillettes* from Troyes are the best known in France. But they are also made in Vouvray, in Châtillon-sur-Loire, Lyon, Châtillon-sur-Chalaronne, Aubagne, Ébreuil, etc.
- Prick each *andouillette* in several places with the point of a knife.
- Place under the broiler.
- Increase the heat gradually. Watch carefully to ensure that the skin becomes golden brown and crackly without burning.

* Small pork sausages made of chitterlings.   Tr.

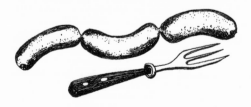

COURTINE'S NOTE: Maigret loves French fried potatoes and usually has them with his *andouillette*. Personally, I prefer a side dish that counterbalances the fat in the sausages, for instance, *cressonnette*.

Here is a recipe for *cressonnette* from the restaurant *La Cloche d'Or:* make a purée of watercress cooked together with long-grain American rice and an onion. Add a little heavy cream and a handful of chopped raw watercress.

With the *andouillette*, Maigret drank *Beaujolais-Villages*.

Soufflé Marie du Port

> The couple arrived at eight o'clock and sat down at once
> because the entrée was a soufflé.
>
> *Maigret on the Defensive*

- Mix 1 cup of minced ham into 2 cups of warm Béchamel sauce. (See Courtine's Note below.)
- Add 1 cup of peeled chopped shrimp and ½ cup of grated Swiss cheese. Add 4 egg yolks one by one.
- Beat 5 egg whites until stiff.
- Add ⅓ of the beaten egg whites into the above mixture, mixing it in well, then gently fold in the rest of the egg whites.
- Thickly butter a soufflé dish.
- Pour in the soufflé mixture (the dish should be about ⅔ full). Place in a moderate oven (325°).
- Bake for about ½ hour, or until the soufflé has puffed up over the rim of the dish.

COURTINE'S NOTE: Here is a recipe for Béchamel sauce. Into a heavy-bottomed saucepan place 2 Tb. of butter, 1 small minced onion, 1 finely chopped carrot, ½ stalk of diced celery, and the chopped white part of 1 leek. Cover and simmer slowly for 10 minutes. Remove the vegetables with a slotted spoon. Place 2 Tb. of butter and ⅓ cup of flour in the pan. Blend and stir with a wooden spoon until the paste is cooked but not brown. Slowly add 3 cups of milk stirring constantly until the sauce comes to a boil. Lower heat, add salt, pepper, a dash of nutmeg, and the vegetables. Cover and cook very slowly for ½ hour, stirring occasionally. Strain.

With the *soufflé Marie du Port*, Maigret drank cider.

Soufflé des Terre-Neuvas

- Soak 2 lbs. of salt codfish for 24 hours. (It wouldn't hurt to change the water a few times—Tr.) Drain the fish, place in a pan, and cover with water. Bring to a boil. Reduce flame and poach gently for 10 minutes.
- Drain the codfish, place on a warm platter, and remove skin and bones. Flake the fish and put the pieces in a saucepan that has been rubbed with garlic.
- Crush the codfish with a wooden spoon. Add some pepper, grated nutmeg, a minced truffle (if procurable—Tr.), and salt (if necessary). Add 2 Tbs. of heavy cream, stir and blend (you can use an electric blender) until a homogeneous mixture is obtained. Place the pan over another pan of slowly simmering water.
- Heat 3½ cups of Béchamel sauce in a saucepan over a low flame. Add 2 egg yolks to the Béchamel, beating them in with a wire whisk.
- Beat 4 egg whites until stiff and fold them into the egg-yolk and Béchamel mixture. (This is the soufflé mixture.)
- In a bowl near (but not *on*—Tr.) the fire, beat 2 egg yolks with 1 Tb. of water. Little by little add, beating all the while, ¾ cup of warm oil. Continue to beat until the product resembles mayonnaise. This is *sauce Mireille*.
- Toast 4 slices of bread.
- On each slice heap 2 Tb. of the warm codfish mixture. On top of this place 4 tsp. of the soufflé mixture. Sprinkle with grated Parmesan cheese. Bake in a hot oven for 6 minutes.
- Place each bread slice on a hot plate. Cover with *sauce Mireille* and serve.

COURTINE'S NOTE: It is important that the codfish is thoroughly de-salted. Salt used in conserving is not the same as salt used in cooking.

With the *soufflé des Terre-Neuvas*, Maigret drank *Gros Plant Nantais*.

Quiche Lorraine

> There was *quiche Lorraine* for supper. He could tell
> by the smell coming from the kitchen.
>
> *Maigret and the Saturday Caller*

- Mix ½ cup of lard, 1 cup of butter, and 1 Tb. of salt with 5 cups
  of all-purpose flour. Add only enough cold water to obtain a soft
  dough, mixing lightly with the hands. Form into a ball and set aside
  in a cool place.
- In a bowl mix 2 cups of heavy cream with 2 eggs. Salt lightly and
  beat until smooth and creamy. In Lorraine, this is called
  "*la migaine.*"
- Roll out the pastry thinly and line a buttered French-style tart pan*
  with it. Prick the dough lightly with a fork.
- Cut about 7 slices of bacon into small pieces and blanch them for a
  few minutes. Drain, wipe, and place on the pastry, pushing the
  pieces of bacon in with the fingers. Place dabs of butter in the spaces
  between the bacon.
- Pour the egg and cream mixture (*la migaine*) on the dough in the
  tart pan and place in a hot oven. Bake for about 25 minutes.
  Check from time to time to see if little "blisters" form on top of
  the *quiche*. If they do, prick them with a fork.
- Remove from oven. Unmold. Let stand 20 minutes before serving.

COURTINE'S NOTE: 2 or 3 tsp. of grated cheese may be added to the
egg and cream mixture.

With the *quiche Lorraine*, Maigret drank *Gris de Toul*.

* See footnote on page 137 for description of this kind of pan.   Tr.

Quiches Tourangelles

"Guess what I've made for you?"

"Quiches!"

It wasn't hard to guess. The whole house was full of their fragrance.

The Flemish Shop

- Make the same pastry as in the preceding recipe, substituting ½ cup butter for the lard. After setting the dough aside for an hour or two, roll it and place it in individual buttered tart pans. Prick the bottom of the pastry in each pan with a fork.
- Place a layer (about ½ inch thick) of *rillettes de Tours* (see below) on the pastry. Sprinkle with finely cut parsley.
- Beat together 4 eggs, ½ tsp. of salt, and ¼ cup of warm milk. Beat in ½ cup of heavy cream and pour into the tart pans.
- Bake in a hot oven (400°) for 20 minutes.

COURTINE'S NOTE: If you would like to make your own *rillettes de Tours*, here is a recipe. Melt 2 lbs. of finely diced pork fat in a heavy pan. Add 9 lbs. of diced fresh pork, salt and pepper, and cook very slowly for 6 hours. When it is lukewarm, place it in a mortar (or heavy bowl) and pound it with a pestle until it is almost pastelike. Put it in little pots. Cover with wax paper.

With the *quiches Tourangelles*, Maigret drank a dry *Vouvray*.

Pizza Napolitaine

> In a side street Maigret chanced upon a little Italian
> restaurant. At the sight of the oven, he was seized
> with a sudden longing for a pizza.
>
> *Maigret and the Loner*

- Make a pizza dough consisting of 2 cups of flour, 1 yeast cake
  (or 1 pkg. dry yeast), ½ cup of water, and a pinch of salt.
  It should look just like bread dough. Let it rise 1 hour in a
  covered bowl.
- Knead the dough for 10 minutes, then pat it out in the shape of a
  circle, 1¼ inches thick. Pinch up the edges around the circle.
- Place on a baking sheet that has been sprinkled with cornmeal.
  Let it stand in a warm place for ½ hour.
- Pour 1⅓ cups of tomato purée on the dough. On top of this place
  ½ lb. of Mozzarella cheese cut in thin strips, the contents of 2 small
  cans of anchovies packed in oil (drain the anchovies), and 3 Tb.
  of pure olive oil. Sprinkle with dried thyme.
- Bake in a hot oven (450°) for about 20 minutes.

COURTINE'S NOTE: Here is a recipe for tomato purée: heat 2 Tb. of
olive oil in a heavy saucepan. Add 1 chopped onion and cook lightly
for a few minutes. Add 3 tomatoes cut in chunks, 3 Tb. of tomato
paste, 1 tsp. of freshly cut basil, and 1 tsp. of sugar. Add salt and
freshly ground black pepper. Simmer slowly, half covered, until the
sauce has thickened. Stir occasionally. Strain and taste for seasoning.

With the pizza, Maigret drank *Chianti*.

Eggs

Oeufs sur le Plat

(*Shirred Eggs*)

Only three or four more years working for other people;
then I'll retire to the little house I've bought in Cagnes
where I'll only cook what I like to eat. *Oeufs sur le plat*
and chops.

Maigret in Montmartre

- Place 1 Tb. of butter in a shallow flameproof dish and heat it in the oven for a few seconds until the butter has melted and the surface of the dish is covered.
- Remove the dish from the oven and break 2 eggs into it.
- Put the dish of eggs in a hot oven (if possible, the heat should come from above rather than from below), for 3 or 4 minutes. Remove dish. Salt the whites and pepper the yolks. Serve in dish.

COURTINE'S NOTE: The size of the dish is very important. If it is too large, the whites of the eggs will spread out and cook before the yolks. Individual dishes of ovenproof porcelain large enough to hold 2 eggs (about 4 inches) are the best.

With his *oeufs sur le plat*, Maigret drank *Domaine des Clairettes* (*Rosé de Provence*).

Omelette aux Fines Herbes

"What will you have to eat? An *omelette aux fines herbes?*"

Maigret Has Doubts

There was a nice juicy *omelette aux fines herbes*, but Maigret didn't even notice it.

Maigret's Boyhood Friend

- Break 6 eggs. Put the yolks in one bowl and the whites in another.
- Beat the yolks with a fork. Continue beating and add 1 Tb. butter cut in bits, salt and pepper. Beat the egg whites until stiff but not dry. Fold the yolks into the whites.
- Melt 2–3 Tb. of butter in a heavy-bottomed frying pan. When it is hot (but not brown), pour in the eggs.
- Holding the handle of the pan with the left hand, tip it slightly, and with the right hand stir the eggs with the back of a fork moving from the sides to the center. When the eggs have reached the consistency of scrambled eggs, move the pan about gently to detach the eggs from the bottom. Continue cooking for a few more seconds.
- Sprinkle the top of the omelet with 3 Tb. of freshly cut parsley, chervil, tarragon, and chives (mixed together).
- Using 2 forks, fold about ⅓ of the omelet toward the center, then fold the opposite side over this.
- Carefully lift the folded omelet onto a warm platter and slip 1 Tb. sweet butter underneath. With a fork pick up another piece of butter and slide it lightly over the surface of the omelet to give it a sheen. Serve.

COURTINE'S NOTE: Any heavy frying pan may be used for omelets, but it should be used *only* for omelets. And it should never be washed. Clean it with paper toweling and coarse salt while it is still warm. If you are afraid of failing with a 6-egg omelet, use 2 smaller pans each holding 3 eggs. A 3-egg omelet is easier to handle.

With the *omelette aux fines herbes*, Maigret drank a dry *Vouvray*.

Omelette de la Fermière

(Peasant Omelette)

> There were three eggs in the henhouse. Maigret insisted
> on making an *omelette*, and she laughed as she watched
> him beating the yolks and the whites of the eggs.
>
> *Maigret se fâche*

- Dice ¼ lb. of smoked ham* and sauté it in melted butter until crisp (2 or 3 minutes). Remove ham and keep it in a warm place.
- Butter 4 ½-inch slices of whole-grain bread and sauté them in the same pan.
- Butter a deep ovenproof pan. Place the slices of sautéed bread in it. Salt and pepper them.
- Separate 6 eggs. Beat the yolks with a fork. Add pepper. Beat the whites until firm but not stiff. Fold the yolks into the whites and pour over the bread slices. Top with the diced ham.
- Put the pan in a hot oven (the heat should come from below rather than above, if possible) for 8 to 10 minutes. Sprinkle with freshly cut parsley and serve.

COURTINE'S NOTE: No salt is needed because the ham gives off salt in cooking.

With the *omelette de la fermière*, Maigret drank a young *Bourgueil*.

* Westphalian or Smithfield ham may be used, or prosciutto.   Tr.

Shellfish

Coquilles Saint Jacques Sautées

(Sautéed Scallops)

> Then he saw her bringing in *coquilles Saint Jacques*,
> a veal roast, and spinach.
>
> > *A Face for a Clue*

- Allow 5 scallops per person. Wash them, dry them in a towel, and sprinkle them with salt and pepper.
- Place some flour on a plate and dredge the scallops in it, shaking the loose flour off each one.
- Heat equal amounts of peanut oil and butter in a heavy frying pan. Turn fire low, add the scallops, and brown them. Cook for 7 to 8 minutes, turning from time to time.
- Drain the scallops and put them on a hot platter. Melt some butter in a saucepan, add the juice of 1 lemon, and pour over the scallops. Sprinkle them with freshly cut tarragon and serve.

With the *coquilles Saint Jacques*, Maigret drank *Vin de Jasnières*.

Coquilles Saint Jacques Grand Langoustier

(*Scallops* Grand Langoustier)

"They've got *coquilles Saint Jacques*. What do you
say to that?"

"*Coquilles Saint Jacques* are all right with me."

Maigret and the Informer

- Sift 3 Tb. of flour on a piece of brown paper and put it in a moderate
  oven until it is light brown in color.
- Sauté 2 large sliced onions in 4 Tb. of pure olive oil. Sprinkle the
  onions with the browned flour and stir with a wooden spoon until
  onions are soft. Add slowly, continuing to stir, 2 cups of dry white
  wine and 2 cups of chicken bouillon.
- Bring this to a boil. Add 1 cup of peeled, seeded, and crushed
  tomatoes, 4 cloves of crushed garlic, 1 spice clove, and a *bouquet
  garni* (see Note, page 15—Tr.). Add salt and pepper. Cook,
  covered, on a low flame for about 1 hour.
- Press sauce through a fine sieve. Place it in a clean pan and bring
  to a boil. Remove from heat. Let stand until lukewarm, then add
  12 shelled green walnuts,* 1 tsp. of crushed capers, and 20 pitted
  black olives. Simmer very slowly for 10 minutes. Set sauce aside.
- Wipe with damp toweling 16 scallops. Place them in a pan, cover
  with cold water, and bring to a boil. Cook 5 minutes. Drain.
- Place the scallops in an ovenproof dish. Cover with ½ cup of dry
  white wine and ½ cup of water to which 1 Tb. of melted butter has
  been added. Salt lightly. Cover the dish with buttered paper and
  bake in a moderate oven for 20 minutes. Drain and place scallops
  on a towel to dry.
- Stiffen the scallops in a little hot olive oil. Drain them again and
  place on a towel to eliminate all traces of oil. Add them to the
  heated sauce and serve.

* If green (undried) walnuts are unobtainable, use the ordinary kind.

COURTINE'S NOTE: The sauce is called *"raïto"* in Provence. It is usually served with poached codfish.

With the *coquilles Saint Jacques Grand Langoustier*, Maigret drank *Vin blanc niçois de Bellet*.

Coquille de Langouste

(Lobster in a Scallop Shell)

> She was already on the landing when he called her back:
> "Bring me a *coquille de langouste!*"
>
> This had been one of his favorite dishes when they were
> poor and he used to linger outside the *charcuterie**
> window.
>
> *Maigret's Little Joke*

- Make a strong court bouillon (see page 37) with Muscadet, or any good dry white wine. Cook a small rock lobster in it. Cool it in the court bouillon.
- Drain the lobster and remove the shell completely. Discard the stomach sack and intestinal vein. Slice the lobster meat in pieces. Remove the lobster coral and pound it in a mortar.
- Steam a carrot, a turnip, ¼ lb. of fresh string beans, and a few asparagus tips. Make a macédoine of these vegetables (cut and mix them). Add some cooked baby shrimp.
- Prepare ¾ cup of mayonnaise for lobster (see page 10), and mix the pounded coral in it. Stir the mayonnaise into the cooled macédoine. Taste for seasoning.
- Place this mixture in 2 deep scallop shells. (If you cannot find real scallop shells, use ovenproof molds; if possible, the kind resembling scallop shells—Tr.) Add the lobster meat, placing the tail slices on top.
- Melt some jellied fish stock. Remove from fire and add a little dry white wine and a pinch of cayenne pepper. When the jelly is lukewarm and on the verge of thickening, spoon it over the lobster mixture.
- Cool. Do not put the shells in the refrigerator until a few seconds before serving.

---

* A French delicatessen in which pork and delicacies made from pork are sold, with a few other delicacies thrown in for good measure. Their show windows very often contain works of high culinary art.   Tr.

COURTINE'S NOTE: Mayonnaise left too long in the refrigerator will decompose.

With the *coquilles de langouste*, Maigret drank *Muscadet de Sèvres-et-Maine tiré sur lie*.

Homard à la Crème

(*Lobster with Cream*)

> He eagerly stuffed a big piece of *homard à la crème*
> in his mouth.
>
> *L'Inspecteur Cadavre*

- Split a live lobster in half lengthwise. Throw away the stomach sack and intestinal vein. Remove and set aside the coral (spongy reddish substance) and the liver. Chop the tail in 2 or 3 pieces and crack the claws.
- Heat 1 Tb. of butter and 1 Tb. peanut oil (or any good cooking oil) in a heavy skillet. Add all the lobster pieces and stir and turn until each piece is red all over. Add salt, pepper, and a pinch of cayenne pepper.
- Add to the lobster pieces 6 Tb. each of cognac and Madeira. Cook briskly until sauce is slightly reduced. Add 1 cup of heavy cream. Lower heat, cover, and simmer for 15 minutes.
- Remove lobster and set tail and claw pieces on a warm platter. (Remove the bits of meat from the carcass and add these to the lobster platter.)
- Pound the coral and liver in a mortar and put them through a sieve. Knead this paste with 2 oz. (½ stick) of butter.
- In a bowl mix 3 egg yolks with 6 Tb. of heavy cream. Add the kneaded butter mixture.
- Add this mixture to the reduced lobster sauce. Place over very low heat, stirring constantly until it is completely blended. Taste for seasoning. Pour over the lobster pieces and serve.

COURTINE'S NOTE: If you like, you can substitute whisky for cognac and vermouth for Madeira.

With the *homard à la crème*, Maigret drank *Haut-Brion blanc*.

Homard à la Mayonnaise

(Lobster with Mayonnaise)

> "What would you say to a *homard à la mayonnaise* for lunch?"
>
> *The Patience of Maigret*

- Make a court bouillon by placing in a deep cooking pot 2 thinly sliced onions and 2 carrots cut in rounds. Add 1 Tb. of coarse salt, 10 peppercorns, a pinch of cayenne pepper, a *bouquet garni* (consisting of parsley, thyme, fennel, and marjoram), 4 cups of water, and a bottle of dry white wine. Bring to a boil. Cover.
- Reduce flame and simmer for ½ hour, then bring to a boil again.
- Plunge a live 2-lb. lobster (for 2 persons), head first, into the boiling court bouillon. Bring to a boil again. Reduce flame and poach for 15 minutes, turning the lobster 2 or 3 times.
- Let the lobster cool in the court bouillon.
- When lukewarm, remove the lobster, split it lengthwise, remove claws, cracking the shells in half with a cleaver. Arrange pieces on a platter and serve with a bowl of mayonnaise for lobster (see page 10).

COURTINE'S NOTE: If you prefer your lobster cold rather than luke-warm, let it stand in a cool place for a while after removing it from the court bouillon. It should never be put in the refrigerator (or, if you insist, only for a few minutes).

With the lobster, Maigret drank *Pouilly-Chasselas*.

Homard à l'Américaine

(Lobster American Style)

> "What do you say we treat ourselves to a *homard*
> *à l'américaine?* And to begin with a big plate of
> *hors d'oeuvres.* Waiter!"
>
> *Maigret's Revolver*

- Place 1 Tb. of olive oil in a small, heavy saucepan. When it is hot, add 2 diced carrots, 1 finely chopped onion, 1 crushed clove of garlic, 1 stalk of finely chopped celery, and a *bouquet garni* (see Note, page 15). Stir and cook for about 5 minutes (the onions should not brown).
- Split lengthwise 2 live Maine lobsters, each weighing about 1½ lbs. Cut the tails in 3 or 4 pieces, and crack the claws with a cleaver. Throw away the stomach sacks (situated near the head) and the intestinal veins (which run along the length of the tail). Take out and set aside the coral (spongy reddish substance) and the liver.
- Place 4 Tb. of olive oil in a heavy skillet and heat until very hot (but not smoking). Add the lobster pieces (in their shells). Salt and pepper them. Cook, stirring, until each piece is red all over. Transfer the cooked pieces to a saucepan and flame with ½ cup of whisky (see Note). Add ½ bottle of dry white wine and bring to a boil.
- Add 3 peeled, seeded, and crushed tomatoes to the boiling mixture.
- Lower heat and add the drained vegetables. Simmer uncovered for 20 minutes.
- Knead ½ cup of butter with 3 Tb. of cornstarch. Still kneading, add the lobster coral, 5 sprigs of freshly cut tarragon, salt, and a good pinch of cayenne pepper. Set aside.
- Remove the lobster pieces from the pan, place on a warm platter, and set in a warm place. Strain the sauce in which the lobster has been cooking through a fine sieve, pushing it with the back of a spoon if necessary.
- Return this to the saucepan, add the butter and coral mixture, and beat with a wire whisk over a low flame until blended. Taste for seasoning. Pour over the lobster pieces and serve.

COURTINE'S NOTE: Whenever possible, use spirits made from grain in cooking. They are far superior to other types of liquor. Pure malt whisky is the best of all!*

With the *homard à l'américaine*, Maigret drank *Puligny-Montrachet* 1967.

* Scotch and Irish whiskies are generally brewed from malted barley.

Mouclade des Boucholeurs

(*Mussels in Cream*)

"Do you like *mouclade?*"

"What is it?"

"Mussels with cream . . . a local dish . . ."

Maigret tried to single out a taste . . . of . . . what could it be? A whiff . . . the barest trace . . .

"Curry!" he cried triumphantly. "I'll bet anything you please there's curry in it! . . ."

La Maison du Juge

- Scrub, scrape, and wash thoroughly 3 qts. of mussels.
- In a large stewing kettle place 1 cup of dry white wine, ½ cup of butter, 8 shallots, 4 crushed cloves of garlic, and a good pinch of pepper. Bring to a boil and add the mussels. Cover.
- Cook several minutes, stirring frequently, until the mussels have opened. Drain the liquid into a saucepan. Bring to a boil, add a pinch of cumin and 2 tsp. of curry powder.* Boil for two minutes.
- Knead 4 Tb. of butter with 2 Tb. of flour. Drop into the boiling liquid, stirring well with a wooden spatula. Remove from fire and add 2 cups of heavy cream. Strain.
- Remove one shell from each mussel. Arrange the mussels in a deep platter. Cover with the sauce and serve.

COURTINE'S NOTE: You can shell the mussels completely—they'll be easier to eat, but it won't look so amusing.

With the *mouclade des boucholeurs*, Maigret drank *Blanc de l'Île de Ré.*

* Monsieur Courtine called for more curry powder. I would add a little at a time, tasting, until it suits you.   Tr.

Fish

Friture de Goujons*

(*Gudgeons Fried in Deep Fat*)

> He crunched the crisp little fish and glanced from time to
> time at the barges moving slowly down the Seine.
>
> *Maigret's First Case*

> Twice during the meal Madame Maigret looked at him
> tenderly. Once when he ordered the *friture de goujons*,
> and again when he asked for *andouille* with a side
> order of French fries.
>
> *Maigret's Little Joke*

- Wipe each fish carefully with a towel.
- One by one dip in beer, then in cornmeal. Shake each fish to
  rid it of loose meal.
- Fry the fish in deep fat, just barely hot. When the fish have turned
  yellow, take them out and drain them. Turn heat up under the oil.
  It should be very hot, but not smoking. Place the fish in the hot oil
  and let them get golden brown.
- Drain the fish on paper toweling. Sprinkle them with salt.
- Pick over, wash, and dry some sorrel leaves. Cut thin rounds of
  lemon. Dip these in fritter batter and fry them in deep fat. Serve the
  sorrel leaves and lemon fritters with the fish.

COURTINE'S NOTE: These fish do not necessarily have to be cleaned.
You can, however, remove the swimming bladder and intestine by
pressing against the abdomen with your thumb.

With the fish, Maigret drank *Blanc de Mennetou-Salon*.

---

* *Goujons* (gudgeons) are a small European fresh-water fish. Smelts or silverfish
can be used to replace them.   Tr.

Raie au Beurre Noir

(Ray in Black Butter)

"Do you think you'll be home for lunch?"

"As far as I know, yes."

"Would you like fish?"

"If you see some *raie*, what about *raie au beurre noir?*"

Maigret Hesitates

- Make a court bouillon with 13 cups of water, 2 cups of wine vinegar, 3 tsp. of coarse salt, 1 tsp. of peppercorns, 1 carrot cut in rounds, 2 sliced onions, and a *bouquet garni* (see Note, page 15). Add a little more parsley to the *bouquet garni* than you do ordinarily. Simmer for 1 hour. Cool.
- Wash half a ray (about 2 lbs.) carefully. Place it in the cold court bouillon. Bring to a boil slowly, skim, and let simmer for 15 minutes.
- Drain the ray. Carefully remove the skin. Wipe the fish with a towel or pat between two sheets of paper toweling. Place it on a very hot platter.
- Put 6 Tb. of butter in a saucepan. Cook slowly until the butter is dark brown. Remove from fire. When it is lukewarm, add 1 tsp. of wine vinegar and 1 Tb. of chopped capers. Heat a moment. Pour over the fish and serve.

COURTINE'S NOTE: In choosing ray, be sure it has little bony, button-like formations under the skin. This is the only kind that will not smell of ammonia.

With the *raie*, Maigret drank *Aligoté*.

44

Maquereaux au Four

(*Baked Mackerel*)

> He had only two hundred yards to go. Then he was home
> breathing in the aroma of *maquereaux au four*. Madame
> Maigret baked them in a slow oven with wine and
> plenty of mustard.
>
> *Maigret and the Killer*

- Clean and score lightly 2 very firm-fleshed fresh mackerel (each
  one weighing about ¾ lb.).
- Chop 3 or 4 shallots and a bunch of parsley together.
- Insert a sprig of thyme, a pinch of pepper, and 1 tsp. of Calvados
  into each fish. Cover the exterior of each fish with a copious layer
  of prepared (Dijon-type) mustard to which some lemon juice has
  been added.
- Spread a layer of the chopped shallot and parsley on the bottom
  of an ovenproof dish and place the mackerel on it. Pour ⅔ cup of
  dry white wine over the fish, cover the dish with a piece of buttered
  paper, and bake in a moderate oven for about 20 minutes.

COURTINE'S NOTE: Mackerel should be eaten as soon as possible after
being caught. A fresh mackerel is very stiff and has bright red gills.

With the *maquereaux au four*, Maigret drank *Muscadet tiré sur lie*.

Sole Dieppoise

> It looked as if what he was staring at were no more
> interesting than a blank wall, and that he was thinking
> of nothing but the *sole dieppoise* he had just ordered.
>
> *Maigret and the Calame Report*

- With the heads, tails, trimmings, etc. of 2 large soles,* make a
  fumet de poisson (concentrated fish stock). Remove and discard
  the dark skin before trimming the fish (that is, before trimming off
  the network of tiny fin bones that run the whole length of the
  contour—Tr.).
- Place the soles, skinned side up, in a shallow flameproof pan,
  along with 4 Tb. of butter and 3 chopped shallots. Pour the *fumet*
  (reduced to ⅓ cup) and ⅔ cup of dry white wine over the fish.
  The liquid should not quite cover the fish. Add salt and pepper.
  Bring to a boil.
- As soon as the liquid boils, cover the pan with buttered paper and
  place in a moderate oven for about 12 minutes.
- Dice 4 large mushrooms and put them in a saucepan with 2 Tb. of
  butter, the juice of 1 lemon, and 4 Tb. of dry white wine. Bring
  to a boil, lower heat, and cook 3 minutes.
- Remove soles from pan with a skimmer and place them on a towel
  to drain. Then set them on a hot platter and put in a warm place.
- Reduce by one-quarter the liquid in which the soles have been
  cooked. Blend 1 Tb. of butter with 2 Tb. of flour and add slowly
  to the liquid. Stir well and shake the saucepan back and forth.
  Add another Tb. of butter, continue to stir, and finally 2 Tb. of
  heavy cream.

* Genuine sole is not available in the U.S., though you may be able to find
deep-frozen imported Dover sole. The most common substitute for European
sole is flounder.   Tr.

- To this sauce add the mushrooms, a handful of baby shrimp, cooked and peeled, and a dozen or so mussels (steamed open in a little dry white wine and some chopped parsley). Taste for seasoning.
- Cover the fish with the sauce and serve.

With the *sole dieppoise*, Maigret drank *Rully*.

Sole Normande

The menu was written on a slate. There was
sole normande and veal roast.

Maigret's Little Joke

His appetite aroused by the smell of the soup, Maigret
dropped into a restaurant famous for its *soles normandes*
and its *tripes à la mode de Caen*.

Les Nouvelles Enquêtes de Maigret

- Melt a piece of butter in a large saucepan over low heat. Add and
  turn lightly the heads, tails, and trimmings of 2 large soles,*
  1 or 2 heads of some other white-fleshed fish, 1 minced carrot,
  1 minced onion, 2 minced shallots, and a *bouquet garni* (see Note,
  page 15). Add 1¼ cups of dry white wine, 3 cups of water,
  2 or 3 chopped mushrooms, and a little salt. Bring to a boil. Skim.
  Cook uncovered for ½ hour. Strain and cool.
- Make a *roux blanc* by blending 2 Tb. of butter and 2 Tb. of flour
  over a low fire. Little by little, add half the fish stock and
  bring to a boil, stirring constantly. Lower heat and cook for ½ hour
  skimming occasionally.
- Scrub, scrape, and wash 1 qt. of mussels. Heat the remaining fish
  stock and add the mussels. Cook briefly (until mussels have
  opened). Remove mussels with a skimmer, take them out of their
  shells, and place them in a bowl. Cover with some of the liquid
  and keep in a warm place.
- Poach ½ pound of raw baby shrimp in the fish stock. Shell them
  and add them to the bowl of mussels. Cook the shrimp shells in
  the stock for 5 minutes.
- Open 12 oysters over a bowl (to catch their liquid). Place the
  oysters in a pan, cover them with the strained oyster liquid, and
  bring to a boil. Remove pan from fire and cool. Skim out the
  oysters, beard them, and put them back in their liquid.

* See note on sole in preceding recipe.   Tr.

- Peel a large truffle. (You will have to resort to canned truffles, or omit this step—Tr.) Cut it in thick slices and place it in a pan containing ¼ cup of dry white wine. Cover the pan with a dampened folded towel and steam for 10 minutes.
- Generously butter a large shallow baking dish and place the sole fillets in it, skinned side up. (You will have already removed and discarded the dark skin and trimmed off the fin bones that edge the fish.) Strain the stock in which the shrimp shells have cooked over the fish. Add the juice of ½ lemon. Dot with butter. Cover the pan with buttered paper and poach gently in a moderate oven for from 15 to 20 minutes (depending on the size of the fish).
- Using great care, place the fish on a large, hot platter. Arrange the mussels and shrimp around them. Decorate the tops of the fish with the oysters and slices of truffle. Cover the platter with the buttered paper previously used and set it near the open oven door.
- Fry 12 smelts in oil, after having first dipped each one in milk, then flour. When they are golden brown, remove them and place on paper toweling to drain.
- Strain the skimmed juice from the poached soles into a saucepan. Beat in 2 egg yolks. Stirring with a wooden spatula, place the pan over a brisk fire and add 4 Tb. of heavy cream. Bring to a boil and remove from fire. Bit by bit add ½ cup of butter, stirring constantly. Heat over a very low flame for a moment. Do not allow to boil.
- Remove the paper covering from the fish and drain off the rendered juice. Cover the fish with the sauce. Arrange the fried smelts around the platter and serve.

COURTINE'S NOTE: In making sauces, use a heavy-bottomed, fairly high pan. The sauce should reach almost to the top of the pan. This will enable you to hold the skimmer horizontally. From time to time, bring the sauce to a brisk boil and skim off the impurities that rise to the surface.

With the *sole normande*, Maigret drank *Corton blanc* 1967.

Rougets Grillés

(*Grilled Red Mullet*)

With the *rougets grillés* they had drunk *Pouilly-fumé*,
the fragrance of which still hovered in the air.

Maigret Hesitates

- Choose small red mullets.* They are usually sold already scaled, and do not need to be cleaned. Trim them. Make several slanting incisions on the fleshy part of the back.
- Brush olive oil over the fish and sprinkle them with herbs (thyme, fennel, rosemary, basil, and marjoram).
- Place the fish on an oiled grill and cook on both sides. Serve with anchovy butter in separate dish.

COURTINE'S NOTE: To make anchovy butter, mix ½ cup of butter with the contents of a small can of drained anchovies. Rub through a sieve.

Of all the aromatic herbs, basil seems to me the most elegant.

With the *rougets grillés*, Maigret drank *Pouilly-fumé*.

* Any small member of the mullet family will do.   Tr.

Chaudrée

(Eel Soup)

> "You'll stay for dinner, Monsieur Maigret? . . .
> I have *mouclade*. . . . I've never forgotten that I was
> born in La Rochelle. My mother had a fish store, so I
> know some good recipes. Have you ever eaten
> *chaudrée fourrassienne?*"
>
> Maigret answered, reciting: "Eel soup with small
> soles and squid."
>
> *Maigret's Pickpocket*

- Have the following fish cleaned and chopped into pieces: 1 small
  conger eel, 3 or 4 small flounders (or some other firm white fish),
  and 3 small squid (the ink sacs must be removed from these latter).
- Place the fish in a stock pot along with 15 cloves of garlic, a
  bouquet garni (see Note, page 15), including some rosemary
  this time. Add 1 bottle of dry white wine and water to cover.
  Salt and pepper.
- Bring to a boil, lower heat, and simmer for 45 minutes.
- Remove *bouquet garni* and place the soup in a tureen. Dot with
  butter. Serve with whole-grain bread.

COURTINE'S NOTE: The garlic should be removed. This is easier to do
if you tie the garlic cloves in a piece of cheesecloth.

With the *chaudrée*, Maigret drank *Domaine de Chevalier* (*Graves
blanc*).

Brandade de Morue

(Salt Cod with Garlic, Cream, and Oil)

> This time it concerned a *brandade de morue*. Pardon had
> telephoned: "Are you free the day after tomorrow?
> Do you like *brandade?* How do you feel about truffles?
> For or against?"
> "For!"
>
> *Maigret's Revolver*

- Freshen a thick 2-lb. piece of salt codfish by leaving it under
  running water all night (or soaking it for 24 hours, changing the
  water as often as practicable).
- Place the fish in a pan of cold water and set over a low flame.
  When foam appears, turn the fire even lower and simmer for
  25 minutes. Drain.
- Skin, bone, and flake the fish.
- Heat ⅔ cup of pure olive oil in a heavy saucepan. When it begins
  to smoke, add the flaked fish. With a wooden spatula, turn and stir
  the fish until it becomes a smooth paste.
- Place the saucepan on the edge of the fire and slowly add 1⅔ cups
  of olive oil, turning and stirring the codfish paste constantly with
  the spatula. From time to time, add 2 Tb. of boiling milk (not more
  than 1 cup in all). Finally, still turning and stirring, add ½ cup
  of heavy cream.
- A successful *brandade* should have the consistency of creamy
  mashed potatoes.
- Carefully brush a black truffle,* chop it, and mix it with the
  brandade. Serve in a deep dish.

COURTINE'S NOTE: Fried croutons slightly rubbed with garlic may be
served with the *brandade.* The dish then becomes Provençal. There is
no garlic in a Languedoc or Nîmes *brandade.*

With the *brandade de morue,* Maigret drank *Hermitage blanc.*

* All will not be lost if you leave the truffle out. Tr.

Aïoli

(Salt Cod with Garlic Mayonnaise)

> "A spot of *marc?*" the innkeeper suggested. "After
> *aïoli* it's a must!"
>
> *The Methods of Maigret*

- Freshen a 2-lb. piece of salt codfish as in previous recipe. Poach
  the fish for 20 minutes. Drain, place on a warm platter, and
  set in a warm place.
- Cook separately 1 lb. of carrots and 1 lb. of fresh string beans.
  Cook (in two waters) a small cauliflower. Bake a large beet.
  Boil 2 lbs. of potatoes in their skins. Peel them and set 2 aside.
- Arrange the vegetables around the codfish.
- Hard-boil 6 eggs. Peel them, cut them in two, and arrange them
  on the platter of codfish and vegetables.
- Clean, then boil 3 dozen snails. Put them back in their shells and
  arrange them on the platter. (You may have to omit this step in
  preparing the dish—Tr.)
- In a large mortar pound 5 whole peeled garlic cloves with 2 tsp. of
  coarse salt. Add 4 egg yolks and the 2 potatoes you have set aside
  and pound to a smooth paste. Continue to pound, adding drop by
  drop, then teaspoon by teaspoon, pure olive oil until the whole
  resembles a mayonnaise (use in all about ½–1 cup of oil).
- Just before serving add the juice of 1 lemon to the sauce. Place
  in a bowl and serve with the platter of codfish.

COURTINE'S NOTE: If your *sauce aïoli* separates (that is, if the oil
rises to the surface), empty out and clean the mortar. Pound a freshly
peeled clove of garlic and slowly add the separated sauce.

With the *aïoli*, Maigret drank chilled red *Château Lacoste*
(*Côteaux d'Aix*).

Omble-Chevalier

(*Lake Trout*)

> He ordered *viande séchée des Grisons* along with ham
> and country sausage, then a lake trout, an *omble-chevalier*.
> *Maigret and the Millionaires*

- Clean and prepare a medium-size lake trout. Split the stomach,
  clip the backbone at each end with a scissors and remove it,
  loosening the small bones with two fingers.
- Cook 3 small carrots in bouillon. Drain. Pick over and cook ½ lb.
  of sorrel. Chop the carrots and sorrel together. Add a large chopped
  truffle (you may have to omit this—Tr.), salt and pepper.
- Stuff the trout with this. Sew up the opening.
- Butter an ovenproof dish. Add a layer of finely chopped shallots
  and place the fish on it. Moisten the fish with some dry white wine.
  Cover the dish with buttered paper and bake in a moderate oven
  (allowing about 10 min. to the pound).
- When baked, place the fish on a hot platter. Remove skin. Set the
  fish in a warm place.
- In a saucepan cook together 2 Tb. of butter and 2 Tb. of flour.
  Add the juice from the fish pan. Stir until blended. Turn heat very
  low. Beat 3 egg yolks in ½ cup of heavy cream and add to the
  sauce, beating it with a wire whisk. Taste for seasoning. Add a dash
  of cayenne pepper and some lemon juice. Pour the sauce over
  the fish and serve.

COURTINE'S NOTE: If the fish stuffing seems too damp, you can add
the inside of white bread soaked in milk (then squeezed out) or a bit
of pounded whiting. Spinach may be substituted for sorrel.

With the *omble-chevalier*, Maigret drank Swiss *Fendant*.

Truites au Bleu

(Brook Trout)

> "Sit down, old man. What do you know! The *Sûreté Nationale* is celebrating too! Put on another place, Georges darling. What would you say to *perdreaux au chou*, you two? You can start with *truites au bleu.* Are they alive and kicking, Georges?"
>
> *Maigret's Special Murder*

- Make a court bouillon using 3 onions, each studded with a clove, 2 carrots cut in rounds, 6 peppercorns, salt, a *bouquet garni* (see Note, page 15), 4 Tb. vinegar, and 1 qt. of water. Boil for 10 minutes.
- Kill 4 live trout with a blow on the head, clean them quickly, sprinkle them with vinegar, and place them in the court bouillon.
- Simmer for 17 minutes. Drain the fish and place on a warm napkin.
- Serve with fried parsley and lemon fritters.

COURTINE'S NOTE: Here is the recipe for the lemon fritters and parsley. Peel lemons and cut them in thin slices. Dip them in thin fritter batter (made with beer) and plunge them into deep hot fat. Drain on paper toweling. Wash and dry a bunch of fresh parsley. Toss it into the hot fat for an instant. Remove and drain.

With the *truites au bleu*, Maigret drank *Sylvaner*.

Tanche au Four

(Baked Fish)

"Old Bambois was here. He sold me a *tanche*
and I baked it. . . ."

Maigret and the Killer

- Make a court bouillon with a bottle of Beaujolais, a sliced onion, a *bouquet garni* (see Note, page 15), salt and pepper. Cool it.
- Clean a good-sized carp, or any firm, white fresh-water fish. Place it in the cold court bouillon. Bring to a boil. Lower heat and simmer for 20 minutes.
- Peel 20 small spring onions. Put them in a saucepan with a lump of butter and a pinch of sugar. Cook over low heat until onions are soft.
- Drain the fish. Place it in an ovenproof dish and surround it with the onions. Put it in a warm place.
- Over high heat reduce the liquid in which the fish has cooked to about ½ cup. Strain. Knead 3 Tb. of butter with 2 Tb. of flour, and stir into the reduced liquid (which has been placed on a very low flame). Add 4 more Tb. of butter, stirring constantly until blended.
- Pour the sauce over the fish and place in a very hot oven for a few minutes.

COURTINE'S NOTE: A few cracklings can be added before serving.

With the *tanche au four*, Maigret drank *Saint-Amour*.

Paella

"I had an excellent *paella* at the *Clou Doré.* . . ."

Maigret Has Doubts

- Boil separately ½ lb. of fresh string beans (cut in half lengthwise) and ½ lb. of fresh green peas.
- Blanch 3 small red peppers and cut them in rounds.
- Grill 6 small pork sausages.
- Scrub and scrape 1 qt. of mussels and steam them open in ⅔ cup of dry white wine to which some pepper has been added.
- Cut up 2 small fresh chickens, preferably grain-fed. (Set aside the giblets, backs, and wings for making the bouillon.) Cut in large dice ½ lb. of lean fresh pork and a small piece of firm white fish.
- Melt 2 Tb. of lard in a large paella pan and brown 2 minced onions in it. Add the chicken pieces, pork, and fish and cook for 20 minutes (turning from time to time).
- Add 2 Tb. of tomato sauce made from fresh tomatoes, ½ tsp. of saffron, salt, pepper, and 1¼ lb. of raw long-grained Carolina rice. Mix with a wooden spoon.
- Remove the pan from the fire and add ½ lb. of shrimp (reserving 6 for later), a few shelled mussels, the beans and peas, the pepper rounds, and the sausages. Add 8 cups of bouillon (made from the giblets and backs of the chicken). Strain in the liquid from the steamed mussels. Cover and place on a hot fire for about 15 minutes.
- Add the 6 remaining shrimp and the rest of the mussels with one shell of each removed. Serve the paella piping hot in the pan in which it was cooked.

COURTINE'S NOTE: The tomato sauce should be very thick and very spicy.

With the *paella*, Maigret drank new *Roussillon* wine.

Game

Becfigues en Brochette*

(*Skewered Game Birds*)

> "How about some little birds for a starter? I have a few
> dozen that were brought in this morning."
>
> *The Methods of Maigret*

- Pluck, then singe the *becfigues*. Do not draw them.
- Arrange them on a platter and pour olive oil over them.
- In a bowl mix bread crumbs with a pinch of nutmeg and a pinch
  each of dried fennel and rosemary crushed to powder. Add salt
  and pepper.
- Roll each bird in this mixture. Wrap each bird in a vine leaf.
  Skewer them, separating one bird from another with a thin piece
  of salt pork or bacon.
- Roast them over an open fire made with vine branches. Catch the
  drippings on slices of stale bread lightly spread with *tapenade*.†

With the *becfigues*, Maigret drank *Châteauneuf-du-Pape*.

* *Becfigues*—small game birds existing only in Provence. They are now protected
by law and may not be hunted. Quail might be prepared in this manner.   Tr.

† *Tapenade*—a coarse purée of black olives pounded in the mortar flavored with
garlic and olive oil. A bit of anchovy fillet or a drop of cognac is sometimes
added. This is a Provençal *hors d'oeuvre*.   Tr.

Perdreaux au Chou

(*Partridges with Cabbage*)

"And the *perdreaux au chou!* Remember? Too bad
it's not the season, because . . ."

Maigret Afraid

- Pluck, draw, and singe 2 fine plump partridges. Truss the feet
  to the body.
- Choose a firm, glossy, well-rounded cabbage. Discard the tough
  outer leaves and cut the cabbage in quarters. Remove the hard
  white center and wash under cold running water.
- Fill a large pot with water and bring to a boil. Add the quartered
  cabbage and boil furiously for 10 minutes. Drain, cool, then, with
  the hands, press out the water.
- Peel a large onion. Scrape and quarter lengthwise 4 large carrots.
- Melt 4 Tb. of butter in a heavy casserole and brown the partridges
  on top of the stove. Take them from the casserole and set aside.
- In the same butter place ½ lb. of lean salt pork cut in small
  chunks and lightly brown them. Add a fresh pork sausage, half
  the cabbage, the carrots, the onion, and a *bouquet garni* (see Note,
  page 15). Place the partridges on this layer and cover with the
  remaining cabbage.
- Add ¾ cup of strong chicken bouillon (or stock), ⅓ cup of dry
  white wine, and 2 Tb. of cognac. Pepper. Cover tightly and cook
  over moderate heat for at least 1 hour.
- Place the cabbage in a deep platter and arrange the halved
  partridges on top. Salt lightly. Surround with the chunks of salt
  pork, the carrot slices, and the sausage (also sliced).
- Bring the liquid in the casserole to a boil and pour it over the
  partridges. Serve.

COURTINE'S NOTE: A lightly smoked sausage may be used in this dish.

With the *perdreaux au chou*, Maigret drank *Santenay, Domaine des
Hautes Cornières.*

Fowl, Rabbit

Canard à la Rouennaise

(*Pressed Duck*)

> For Maigret it all began in a perfectly ordinary way one evening when they were having dinner at the Pardons.
>
> Madame Pardon had prepared a *canard au sang* which she made to perfection, and which was one of the *commissaire*'s favorite dishes.
>
> *Maigret in Vichy*

- Salt and pepper the inside of a duck (or duckling).
- Roast it in a very hot oven for 16–18 minutes. The meat should not be too cooked, in fact, when the duck is pricked with a fork the juices should run red.
- Put ½ bottle of red wine and 1 tsp. of minced shallot in a saucepan. Simmer slowly to syrup consistency.
- Remove duck from the oven and skin it. Detach the legs, coat them with prepared mustard, and finish cooking them under the broiler.
- Cut the breast meat in thin slices. Place these on a hot platter and cover.
- Cut up the carcass, chop it, and press it in a duck press catching the blood in a bowl.
- Press the raw duck liver through a sieve. Knead the liver "purée" with 6 Tb. of butter. Little by little add the blood and incorporate this mixture into the thickened wine. Taste for seasoning. Sprinkle with nutmeg. Heat over a very low flame.
- Arrange the strips of breast meat on a hot platter, placing a leg at each end. Cover with sauce. Serve.

COURTINE'S NOTE: It is indispensable that the duck be strangled rather than butchered, so that none of the blood is lost.

Mashed turnips go very nicely with this dish.

With the *canard à la rouennaise*, Maigret drank *Corton-Grancey*.

Caneton à l'Orange

(Duckling with Orange Sauce)

> "Will you be eating here? We have *caneton à l'orange*.
> You can begin with two or three dozen scallops that
> just came in from La Rochelle. . . ."
>
> *Maigret's Pickpocket*

- Braise a duckling weighing 2½–3 lbs. in butter for about ½ hour over low heat. At the end of this time pour ¼ cup of Grand Marnier over it. Simmer for 5 minutes. Remove from pan, cover with aluminum foil, and set in a warm place.
- Strain the juice into a saucepan. Add 1 Tb. of white wine vinegar, 1 Tb. of sugar, the juice of 3 oranges, and ½ cup of strong chicken stock (or bouillon). Simmer gently for 10 minutes. Skim off fat. Strain.
- Taste sauce for seasoning. Add 3 tsp. of Mandarin (or any good orange liqueur—Tr.).
- Put 4 peeled, quartered, and seeded oranges in a small saucepan. Moisten with 2 or 3 Tb. of the duckling sauce. Bring to a boil. Remove from stove.
- Place the duckling on a hot platter. Surround it with the quartered oranges and the sauce the oranges were cooked in. Place the rest of the sauce in a bowl. Serve.

COURTINE'S NOTE: Be sure to get a very young duckling, not a duck. Use only unsprayed oranges, even if the skin is not used.

With the *caneton à l'orange*, Maigret drank *Tavel*.

Canard à l'Orange

(Duck with Orange Sauce)

> In the end they chose cold Vichyssoise and *canard à l'orange* which was the specialty of the day.
>
> *Maigret on the Defensive*

- Singe a cleaned 4–5 lb. duck (or duckling) over a gas or spirit flame and wipe carefully with a towel. Truss it.
- Peel, seed, and chop an orange, setting the peel to one side. Place the orange pieces inside the duck and sew up the opening.
- Melt 4 Tb. of butter in a heavy casserole. When it is hot, put in the duck and brown it for about 20 minutes. Salt and pepper the duck. Add the orange peel cut in strips, ½ cup of dry white wine, and ⅔ cup of stock (or bouillon). Cover and cook slowly for 1 hour.
- Cut the peel of 2 oranges into thin strips and blanch for 3 minutes.
- Take the duck out of the casserole and set it in a warm place. Put the juice of the 2 peeled oranges into the casserole and deglaze it by scraping the coagulated juices up from the bottom with a wooden spatula. Add the orange peel, a pinch of sugar, and ¼ cup of Curaçao. Place pan on fire and bring to a boil.
- Carve the duck, first removing the legs. Place it on a hot platter. Pour some of the sauce over it. Decorate the platter with segments of peeled oranges. Serve the rest of the sauce separately.

COURTINE'S NOTE: The duck may be served whole and carved at the table.

With the *canard à l'orange*, Maigret drank *Château Giscours (Margaux)*.

Coq au Vin Blanc

(*Chicken in White Wine*)

"I've always wondered how you made it. . . ." She was
referring to the *coq au vin* they had eaten for dinner.
Madame Pardon went on: "There's a faint aftertaste,
you hardly notice it, that makes it so delicious.
I don't know what it is."

"It's simple . . . I suppose you add a glass of cognac
to yours at the last minute?"

"Cognac or armagnac, whatever I happen to have. . . ."

"There you are! I add *prunelle d'Alsace*, though I know
it's not in the cookbooks. That's the whole secret. . . ."

Maigret Has Doubts

They ate *rillettes du pays*, a *coq au vin blanc*, and after
the goat cheese, they had *babas au rhum*.

Maigret and the Killer

- Peel, wash, and slice 3 carrots and 1 leek. Peel and chop 1 onion
  and 4 shallots. Peel and crush 2 cloves of garlic. Wash a sprig of
  parsley. Disjoint a 4–4½ lb. cockerel (or a good roasting
  chicken—Tr.). Hold the feet over an open flame for a moment
  in order to be able to remove the scaly skin that covers them.
- Place one of the carrots, the leek, the onion, the parsley, and the
  chicken feet in a saucepan. Add ½ bay leaf and a sprig of thyme.
  Add 1¼ cups of water. Cook slowly for about ½ hour, or until
  the liquid is reduced to about ⅓ cup. Strain.
- Put some lard in a heavy Dutch oven and brown the chicken pieces
  in it. Remove them. In the same pan place the rest of the carrots,
  the shallots, and the garlic. Lower the flame and cook for 10 minutes
  (until slightly brown).
- Put back the chicken pieces. Sprinkle them with 1 Tb. of flour.
  Stir until flour is absorbed. Add the strained bouillon and ⅓ cup
  of Riesling (or other dry white wine—Tr.). Add a sprig of thyme,
  a pinch of grated nutmeg, salt and pepper. Cover and simmer gently
  for an hour, or until tender.

- Squeeze the juice from ½ lemon. In a bowl beat 1 egg yolk with ⅓ cup of heavy cream.
- When the chicken is done place the pieces in a hot serving dish. Off heat, add the egg and cream mixture to the chicken sauce in the pan. Then add the lemon juice and 1 Tb. of *eau de vie de prunelle* (plum brandy). Pour over the chicken and serve.

COURTINE'S NOTE: A good accompaniment to this dish is homemade noodles.

With the *coq au vin blanc*, Maigret drank *Riesling*.

Coq au Vin Rouge

(*Chicken in Red Wine*)

> He went home for lunch. His wife had made one of his
> favorite dishes—*coq au vin.*
>
> *Maigret and the Loner*

- Cut ¼ lb. of lean bacon into thin pieces. Peel 24 small white onions.
  Disjoint a 5–6 lb. rooster (or a good roasting chicken—Tr.).
- Melt 3 Tb. of lard in a Dutch oven. Add the pieces of bacon and
  cook them for 10 minutes. Add the onions and brown them (for
  about 10 minutes), stirring from time to time. Remove the bacon
  and onions with a slotted spoon and set aside. Put the pieces of
  chicken in the pan, a few at a time, and brown them carefully
  on all sides. Allow about 20 minutes for this.
- Meanwhile heat a bottle of red wine to which 1 lump of sugar
  has been added.
- Place all the browned chicken pieces in the Dutch oven. Add salt,
  pepper, and 5 Tb. *marc* (brandy). Flame. Remove chicken pieces.
- Return the onions and bacon to the Dutch oven. Sprinkle them
  with 2 Tb. of flour and stir until all the flour is absorbed. Add the
  chicken, then the wine.
- Add 1 peeled, chopped clove of garlic, a sprig of thyme (or a pinch
  of dried thyme), a sprig of parsley, and a bay leaf. Cover and
  simmer for 1½ hours or until tender.

COURTINE'S NOTE: A good full-bodied wine should be served with
this dish.

Maigret drank *Châteauneuf-du-Pape* with his *coq au vin.*

Poulet Rôti

(*Roast Chicken*)

> The room was fragrant with simmering soup and there
> was already a larded roast chicken on the table.
>
> *Maigret's Special Murder*

- Choose a medium-sized roasting chicken. Season the inside
  sparingly with salt and pepper and add the giblets. Truss it and
  cover it with strips of bacon (previously simmered for 10 minutes).
- Heat oven to moderate. Place chicken on the roasting rack and
  roast it for about 1 hour and 20 minutes. Baste it from time to time
  with the juice in the roasting pan.
- About 5 minutes before chicken is done, remove the bacon slices
  so as to brown it completely.
- Pour the juice into a warm bowl and remove the fat that has risen
  to the surface with a skimmer.
- Deglaze the roasting pan by placing it over a brisk fire, adding
  3 or 4 tsp. of hot water and scraping up the coagulated juices
  with a wooden spatula. Add this to the degreased juice.

COURTINE'S NOTE: To avoid overcooking the white meat you can
remove the chicken from the oven before it is quite done and carve it.
Put the legs back in the oven for another 2 or 3 minutes.

With the roast chicken, Maigret drank *Pomerol*.

Poulet Bonne Femme

> When he came home there was a *poulet bonne femme*
> ready for him and a Madame Maigret who was sorry
> for what she'd said that morning.
>
> *Maigret's Little Joke*

- Salt and pepper (inside as well as out) a medium-size roasting chicken. Place it in a heavy pan with 4 Tb. of butter and brown it. Turn it and baste it frequently until it is about half cooked.
- Blanch 2 oz. (⅓ cup) of diced lean bacon for 10 minutes. Drop 20 small peeled white onions into boiling water and boil them for a few minutes. Peel 2 lbs. of small boiling potatoes. Trim them into ovals of olive size.
- Arrange the bacon, onions, and potatoes around the half-cooked chicken; they should cover the bottom of the pan, so that the contents get slightly browned. Put the pan, uncovered, in a fairly hot oven and bake for about 1 hour.
- Taste for seasoning. Sprinkle freshly cut parsley over the chicken and serve it in the same pan in which it was cooked.

COURTINE'S NOTE: It is very important to use a real farm chicken for this dish!

With the *poulet bonne femme*, Maigret drank *Saint-Nicolas-de-Bourgueil.*

Poule au Pot

(*Boiled Chicken*)

> The chicken was on the fire along with a beautiful red
> carrot, a big onion, and a knob of parsley with the
> stalks sticking out.
>
> *Madame Maigret's Own Case*

- Have a good-sized roasting chicken prepared for stuffing.
- Chop the chicken liver along with 3 other chicken livers with ½ lb.
  of smoked ham (Westphalian ham or prosciutto will do—Tr.).
- Beat 3 eggs. Add salt, pepper, a dash of nutmeg, 2 chopped shallots,
  ½ clove of crushed garlic, a sprig of parsley and a sprig of
  tarragon cut with scissors, and a thick slice of stale bread that has
  been soaked in milk. Add the chopped livers and ham and mix
  well, using your hands.
- Stuff the chicken with this mixture. Sew up the opening. Wrap a
  wide thin piece of ham fat (previously simmered for 10 minutes)
  around the chicken.
- Pour 3 qts. of water in a large pot and add the gizzard and feet
  of the chicken. When the water boils put in the chicken, bring
  to a boil again, add salt and skim. Cover and cook over low heat
  for 1 hour.
- Add 4 carrots, 3 turnips, 1 white part of leek, a large onion studded
  with 2 cloves, 1 stalk of celery, 1 unpeeled clove of garlic, and
  some sprigs of parsley tied together. Continue cooking for
  1½ hours.
- Remove the wrapping of fat from the chicken. Place the chicken
  on a hot platter surrounded with the vegetables.

COURTINE'S NOTE: You might start with the chicken broth. Strain it
and pour it over slices of toasted whole-grain bread spread very
lightly with strong mustard.

With the *poule au pot*, Maigret drank *Madiran*.

Poule en Daube en Gelée

(Braised Chicken in Aspic)

> He found a chicken leg still coated with glossy aspic.
> He cut himself a thick slice of bread and buttered it.
> . . . "Tell me . . ."
>
> He went into the house, munching: "You wouldn't
> happen to have some beer?"
>
> *L'Inspecteur Cadavre*

- Put a calf's foot split in half in a soup pot (preferably an earthenware *marmite*) along with 4 onions, 4 carrots cut in rounds, ½ lb. of diced lean bacon (previously simmered for 10 minutes), and a *bouquet garni* (see Note, page 15). Cover with cold water, to about half the height of the *marmite*. Add salt. Bring to a boil and simmer, covered, for ½ hour.
- Cut the legs from a good-sized young chicken. Place these and the rest of the chicken in the pot. Bring to a boil. Skim. Cover and cook for ½ hour.
- Add ½ bottle of dry white wine, and simmer, covered, for 1½ hours.
- Add 5 Tb. of cognac or armagnac, some ground pepper, a clove, a pinch of allspice, and simmer covered for another ½ hour.
- Remove the chicken from the pot. Cut the second joints from the drumsticks and the rest of the chicken into serving pieces. Arrange on a deep platter. Distribute the diced bacon between the pieces of chicken.
- Strain the cooking juice and let it stand for about 15 minutes. Skim off fat. Place on a low flame and reduce until thoroughly thickened. Taste for seasoning. Pour over the chicken pieces, making sure that only a thin layer coats each piece. Cool and place in the refrigerator.

COURTINE'S NOTE: The calf's foot boned and warmed in a little of the jelly that has been set aside and served with an oil, vinegar, and herb dressing makes an excellent *hors d'oeuvre*.

With the *poule en daube en gelée*, Maigret drank beer.

Pintadeau en Croûte

(*Guinea Fowl in Crust*)

> The dinner had been especially successful. Madame
> Maigret had prepared *pintadeau en croûte* and the
> *commissaire* had brought up from the cellar one of the
> last bottles from a case of old *Châteauneuf-du-Pape*
> he had bought at an auction one day when he happened
> to be on the Rue Drouot.
>
> *Maigret and the Informer*

- Make a stuffing by mixing the liver of the guinea fowl with a small chopped lamb kidney, some *foie gras*, salt, pepper, and 1 Tb. of cognac. Cover 2 large fresh truffles (you will have to resort to canned truffles—Tr.) with this mixture and stuff the fowl. Sew up the opening. Truss the bird.
- Put some butter in a casserole and brown the fowl. Cook it slowly until it is about three-quarters done.
- Make *pâte feuilletée* (or use ready-made puff paste, which can be purchased frozen—Tr.). Roll out as thinly as possible.
- Wrap the fowl generously in the *pâte feuilletée* and finish cooking in a medium hot oven (about 15 minutes). Serve.

COURTINE'S NOTE: A *sauce Périgueux* may be served with the guinea fowl in crust: to 1 cup of brown sauce add ¼ cup of Madeira, 1 minced truffle (optional), ¼ cup of minced prosciutto, a pinch of thyme, and ¼ bay leaf. Heat very slowly. Then add 1 Tb. of butter and 2 more Tb. of Madeira.

With the *pintadeau en croûte*, Maigret drank *Châteauneuf-du-Pape*.

Lapin de Chou Farci

(*Stuffed Rabbit*)

"What do you think of this rabbit?"

"It's excellent."

"A little *marc* to wash it down? On me this time."

Maigret Goes to School

- Prepare a large domestic rabbit for roasting and stuffing. Stuff it with its own liver, chopped, and 2 *pieds de porc truffés en crépine*.* Sew up the opening.
- Brush the rabbit with strong mustard and place it in a marinade consisting of dry white wine, 2 sliced onions, 2 minced carrots, a sprig of thyme, a bay leaf, a few parsley sprigs, and 1 Tb. of *marc* (brandy). Marinate the rabbit for 48 hours basting from time to time with the marinade.
- Drain the rabbit and weigh it. Allow 20 minutes per pound for baking. Place it in a hot oven until done, basting it now and then with the marinade.
- Serve the cooking juice in a separate bowl.

COURTINE'S NOTE: Saltless mustard, such as recommended by dieticians, may be used.

With the *lapin farci*, Maigret drank red *Saint-Pourçain*.

* Pig's feet, boned, "truffled," and wrapped in caul fat. My market-lady tells me these are great delicacies and in Paris sold only at Christmastime.   Tr.

Sauté de Lapin de Garenne

(Sautéed Wild Rabbit)

> A few minutes later he pushed the door open with a
> familiar movement, sniffing the kitchen smells as he did
> every evening.
>
> There was a *lapin de garenne* for dinner, a rarity these
> days. A friend with a farm at Cléry had organized a hunt
> the day before to do away with the hundreds of rabbits
> which had been seriously damaging his crops.
>
> *Les Nouvelles Enquêtes de Maigret*

- Skin, clean, and cut a young wild rabbit (about 3 lbs.) into pieces.
- Heat 2 Tb. butter and 3 Tb. cooking oil in a heavy pan. Add the
  pieces of rabbit seasoned with salt and pepper and brown them
  on all sides.
- Drain off the fat and sprinkle the rabbit pieces with flour. Turn
  them until the flour is absorbed. Add 4 cups of strong veal broth
  (or bouillon), 1 Tb. of tomato paste, and a *bouquet garni* (see
  Note, page 15). Bring to a boil and simmer for 1 hour.
- Lift out the rabbit pieces and place them in a clean casserole.
  Place a thick layer of homemade noodles, previously boiled for
  8 minutes in salted water, on top of the rabbit pieces.
- Strain the liquid in which the rabbit has cooked into a saucepan.
  Cook it until it has reduced to about 2 cups. Remove from fire and
  stir in 1 cup of heavy cream. Taste for seasoning.
- Pour this sauce over the noodles and simmer very slowly for
  15 minutes.

COURTINE'S NOTE: Here is Madame Maigret's recipe for ½ lb. of
noodles. Mix 2 cups of sifted flour with 2 eggs and a pinch of salt.
Knead well and set aside for 1 to 2 hours. Roll the dough thinly into
rectangular sheets. Fold the sheets in two and hang them over an
improvised clothesline. Let them dry for at least an hour before
cutting and cooking them.

With the *lapin de garenne*, Maigret drank *Chambolle-Musigny*.

Variety Meats—
Tripe, Calf's Head,
Kidney, Liver, etc.

Rognons d'Agneau au Madère

(Lamb Kidneys in Madeira)

> "Would you mind telling me what you had to eat?"
> With feigned ill-humor, he replied: *"Rognons d'agneau."*
> *Maigret and the Headless Corpse*

- Remove the skin from 6 lamb kidneys (for two persons). Cut them in half and carefully cut out the sinews (or ask your butcher to do this). Wash them thoroughly under cold running water. Dry them and slice in thin strips.
- Wash, or wipe, and chop ⅔ cup of mushrooms. Cook slowly in 1 Tb. of butter.
- Heat 2 Tb. of butter in a heavy frying pan. Add the kidney slices and cook them over high heat, stirring constantly, until they turn a pale gray (a matter of 5 or 6 minutes). Salt them and place them in a covered dish on top of a pan of hot water.
- Mince 1 shallot. Heat the pan in which the kidneys were cooked. Add the minced shallot, stirring briskly. Stir in 2 Tb. of Madeira, some ground pepper, a sprig of thyme, and the chopped mushrooms with their juice. Simmer for a few minutes. Taste for seasoning. Bring to a boil, stirring, then pour over kidneys. Sprinkle with freshly cut parsley and serve.

COURTINE'S NOTE: Port or sherry may be substituted for Madeira.

With the *rognons d'agneau au madère*, Maigret drank *Hermitage rouge*.

Tripes à la Mode de Caen

> He took him to Les Halles and ordered *tripes à la mode de Caen* and *crêpes Suzette* that were served in a pretty copper chafing dish.
>
> *The Methods of Maigret*

> The *tripe* was delicious, and when Maigret left the table he was in a state of bliss topped off by the fact that he hadn't had the strength to refuse the *Calvados* that was a specialty of the house.
>
> *Les Nouvelles Enquêtes de Maigret*

- Cut 8–9 pounds of washed and blanched tripe.into 2-inch squares. Cut 3 carrots in quarters, slice 10 onions, and make 2 *bouquets garnis* (see Note, page 000), only this time add 2 bay leaves to each *bouquet* and a little extra parsley.
- Rub the inside of a large earthenware casserole with garlic. Place ⅓ of the tripe pieces on the bottom. Salt them lightly, pepper them abundantly. Then add ⅓ of the carrots and onions, one of the *bouquets garnis*, and ½ of a washed and blanched calf's foot that has been split in two.
- Add another layer of tripe, then the remaining carrots and onions and the other piece of calf's foot, the second *bouquet garni*, and finish with a last layer of tripe.
- Add ⅓ cup of Calvados (apple jack) and 3⅓ cups of hard cider.
- Cover the casserole and seal it hermetically with a thick paste made of flour and water.
- Bake in a slow oven for about 10 hours.
- Break the cooked paste and take off cover. With a skimmer remove *only* the pieces of tripe. Place them in a hot serving dish. Strain the juice over them and serve. Or cool and reheat for serving.

TRANSLATOR'S NOTE: The tripe available in America is called honey-comb tripe. It is ready for cooking. Be sure you buy fresh honeycomb tripe and not pickled tripe (which is so labeled). Prepare the tripe within one or two days of buying it. Cooking time for this tripe can be reduced to 4–5 hours.

With the *tripes à la mode de Caen*, Maigret drank cider.

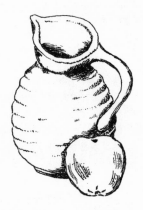

Tête de Veau en Tortue

(Calf's Head Turtle Fashion)

"Are you free tomorrow evening?"

"Yes."

"Do you like *tête de veau en tortue?*"

"I never ate it."

"Do you like *tête de veau?*"

"Pretty well."

"Then you'll like it *en tortue*. It's a dish I discovered on a trip to Belgium. You'll see. Come to think of it, I don't know what wine to serve with it . . . Maybe beer . . ."

At the last minute, after an almost scientific explanation, Pardon settled for a light *Beaujolais*.

Maigret's Revolver

- Soak in cold water half a calf's head (purchased trussed and blanched) and 1 calf's tongue.
- Half-fill a large cooking pot with water. Add salt, pepper, 1 large onion studded with 2 cloves, and the juice of 2 lemons. Bring to a boil. Add the calf's head and the tongue and boil gently for about 2 hours.
- A half hour before the cooking is completed, remove the tongue and skin it. Put it back with the head and finish cooking.
- Soak a calf's brain for 1 hour in water to which some vinegar has been added. Skin it and remove the membranes.
- Prepare a court bouillon with a *bouquet garni* (see Note, page 15), an onion studded with a clove, 1 Tb. of vinegar, and a pinch of salt. Heat. When the water is lukewarm, put in the brain. Bring to a boil, lower heat, and cook 20 minutes. Remove the brain, drain it, and keep it hot over warm water.
- Soak 1 cup of green olives in cold water for ½ hour (to rid them of salt). Pit them. Cut 6 gherkins in thin rounds. Hard-boil 3 eggs.

- Place ¾ cup of mellow white wine in a saucepan with 1 tsp. of sage, ¼ tsp. of marjoram, ¼ tsp. of rosemary, ½ tsp. of basil, ¼ tsp. of thyme, 1 tsp. of dried bay leaf, and a few parsley leaves. Simmer until reduced by half. Turn off fire, let the brew stand for a while, then strain.
- Dice ¼ lb. of Italian-type ham and mince 2 carrots. Sauté lightly in a little butter. Sprinkle with flour, stir until brown, then add the strained herb brew and 4 cups of the veal bouillon. Cover and simmer for 30 minutes.
- Add the pitted olives, the gherkins, and 3 Tb. of tomato paste. Cover and simmer for 20 minutes.
- Cut the calf's head in pieces. Slice the tongue and the brain. Place the meat on a hot platter. Cover with the sauce and decorate the platter with the hard-boiled eggs cut in halves. Serve.

COURTINE'S NOTE: Theoretically, this dish should be served with dumplings made of sweetbreads, giant shrimp, and croûtons. But is it necessary? The housewife, like Madame Maigret, will hesitate.

With the *tête de veau en tortue*, Maigret drank Belgian beer.

Tête de Veau à la Sainte Ménéhould

(Calf's Head St. Ménéhould Style)

> He glanced over the mimeographed menu, then handed it
> to Janvier. "I'll have the *tête de veau*. . . ."
>
> *Maigret in Court*

- Place half a calf's head under cold running water for an hour. This will rid it of its blood and whiten it.
- Cook until tender in a *blanc* (see Courtine's Note below—Tr.). Drain.
- While the meat is still warm, cut into 2-inch pieces and place them in a bowl.
- In another bowl beat ⅓ cup of oil with the juice of 1 lemon. Add salt and pepper and pour over the meat. Marinate for 1 hour.
- Remove the pieces of meat one by one. Wipe them dry.
- Melt ½ cup of butter in an open oven pan. Place 2 cups (more if necessary) of dry bread crumbs on a plate.
- Dip each piece of meat first into the butter, then coat with the breadcrumbs. Repeat operation so that each piece of meat has been coated with butter then with breadcrumbs twice.
- Place the pieces of meat under a hot grill and brown. Serve with mustard or mustard sauce.

COURTINE'S NOTE: To make a *blanc*, blend 2 heaping Tb. of flour with some cold water. Strain this mixture through a fine sieve and put it in a large cooking pot. Add 9 cups of water, 1 Tb. of salt, and 2 tsp. of vinegar. Bring to a boil. Add an onion studded with a clove, a *bouquet garni* (see Note, page 15), and the calf's head tied up in a piece of cheesecloth.

With the *tête de veau à la Sainte Ménéhould*, Maigret drank *Vin gris de Toul*.

Ris de Veau Grand-Mère

(*Sweetbreads Grandmother's Style*)

> "How was her appetite?"
>
> "Let me see . . . a dozen snails . . . sweetbreads, cheese, strawberries and cream. . . ."
>
> *The Most Obstinate Man in Paris*

- Choose 2 very white sweetbreads. Place them under slowly running cold water for 3 hours.
- Put them in a pot of cold salted water and bring to a boil. Blanch them for 3 minutes. Drain. Cool them thoroughly in cold water. When they are cold and firm, drain and remove the cartilage, veins, connective tissue, and fat. Do NOT remove the fine membrane around them.
- Wrap the sweetbreads in a towel, place them on a plate, and put a weight on them.
- Lard each sweetbread with 2 oz. of salt pork (previously simmered for 10 minutes) cut in thin strips, and the same amount of cooked smoked tongue.
- Brown the sweetbreads in butter. Remove them from the skillet with a slotted spatula. Deglaze the pan by adding ⅓ cup of dry white wine and scraping up the coagulated juice with a wooden spatula. Mince 3 carrots and 2 small turnips. Place these in the pan. Salt and pepper them. Place the sweetbreads on top of the vegetables and cover with 1 cup of veal stock.
- Cover and bring to a boil. Turn down flame and cook until tender. Place the sweetbreads on a hot platter along with the juice and vegetables.

TRANSLATOR'S NOTE: Sweetbreads are highly perishable and should be cooked within twenty-four hours of purchasing.

With the *ris de veau grand-mère*, Maigret drank *Château Poujeaux* (*Moulis-Médoc*).

Ris de Veau à la Belge

(Sweetbreads Belgian Style)

> They savored their sweetbreads which were delicious.
> Then they had tiny chops, and for dessert
> *gâteau aux fraises.*
>
> > *Maigret and the Madwoman*

- Prepare 2 sweetbreads as in preceding recipe.
- Cut them in thick slices. Salt and pepper them and dip them in flour.
- Melt some butter in a heavy skillet. When the butter foams, add the sweetbreads and cook slowly for about 10 minutes. When they are nearly done, add 1 Tb. of butter and 3 finely chopped shallots.
- Place the sweetbreads on a hot platter and sprinkle them with freshly cut chives and tarragon. Pour foaming butter over them.
- Surround the platter with fresh vegetables: green peas, broccoli, asparagus tips, carrots and turnips cut in ovals, and artichoke bottoms (each vegetable cooked separately, then braised).

COURTINE'S NOTE: In Belgium, sweetbreads are often garnished with hop shoots when they are in season—delicious.

With the *ris de veau à la belge*, Maigret drank a *Moselle*.

Foie de Veau en Papillotes

(Veal Liver in Paper)

> Deep in thought, he ate his *foie de veau en papillotes.* . . .
>
> *Maigret and the Bum*

> "Will you have mackerel?"
>
> "And some *foie de veau en papillotes* . . ."
>
> It was mostly the liver that tempted him. That and the
> atmosphere of the brasserie where he hadn't set foot
> for weeks.
>
> *Maigret Loses His Temper*

- Marinate 2 thick slices of calf's liver in olive oil to which has been added salt, pepper, nutmeg, and a bay leaf.
- Make a stuffing consisting of 1 cup of fresh bread pulp, 3 Tb. freshly cut herbs (chives, parsley, tarragon, and chervil), 1 chopped mushroom, and some salt and pepper.
- Coat the liver slices with this mixture. Then wrap each slice in a thin slice of caul fat (see Note under *Pâté de Campagne*, page 14). Cut into heart shapes 2 pieces of heavy well-oiled wax paper and fold around each slice.
- Place on a hot griddle. Cook 5 minutes on each side. Serve.

COURTINE'S NOTE: Choose the liver carefully. It should be fine-grained and light-colored.

With the *foie de veau en papillotes*, Maigret drank *Châteauneuf-du-Pape*.

Foie de Veau à la Bourgeoise

(*Veal Liver Bourgeois Style*)

> *Foie de veau à la bourgeoise* . . . one of his favorite dishes.
>
> "Have you made enough so we can have it tomorrow as a *hors d'oeuvre?*"
>
> It was a dish he liked best cold, the day after. . . .
> *Maigret and the Wine Merchant*

- Marinate for ½ hour 2 lbs. of calf's liver in 2 cups of water to which 1 Tb. of vinegar, a *bouquet garni* (see Note, page 15), 1 onion studded with a clove, and 1 Tb. of olive oil have been added. Turn occasionally. Drain and wipe.
- Melt some butter in a deep skillet. Brown 4 ounces of lean bacon (previously simmered for 10 minutes), cut in thin strips. Add the liver and carefully brown it on all sides. Add 20 small white pearl onions and ½ cup of very fresh small mushroom caps. Pour in 1 Tb. of brandy, 1 or 2 Tb. of the marinade, and 1 cup of veal bouillon. Cover and simmer for 1½ hours. Cut in slices and serve, along with the onions and mushrooms.

COURTINE'S NOTE: If too much liquid is left in the skillet, reduce until thick, and pour it over the liver.

With the *foie de veau à la bourgeoise*, Maigret drank *Santenay, Domaine des Hautes Cornières*.

Meat

Ragoût de Boeuf au Paprika

(Beef Stew with Paprika)

> What a nice Sunday! A beef stew simmering in the
> low-ceilinged, blue-tiled kitchen, the whole house
> fragrant with the scent of herbs . . .
>
> *The Patience of Maigret*

- Place 2 Tb. of butter in a Dutch oven. Add ¼ lb. of diced fat trimmed from fresh ham and cook until the fat has melted.
- Cut 2½ lbs. of rump of beef into 1–2-inch pieces. Chop 1 lb. onions coarsely.
- Place a layer of meat in the bottom of the pan. Salt it and cover it with half the chopped onions. Add ½ tsp. of paprika.
- Add the rest of the meat, the onions, salt, and another ½ tsp. of paprika. Add ¾ cup of hot water. Bring to a boil, lower heat, and simmer covered for 2 hours and 45 minutes.
- At the end of cooking time add 1 cup of heavy cream. Bring to a boil, remove from stove, and serve.

COURTINE'S NOTE: As a change from the usual steamed potatoes, this dish can be served with potted red cabbage. Shred a large red cabbage (about 2 lbs.) and place it in a heavy saucepan with ½ cup of butter. Salt and pepper the cabbage. Simmer slowly for ½ hour, then sprinkle with flour and add ¾ cup of red wine. Simmer covered until all the wine has been absorbed (about 2 hours).

With the *ragoût de boeuf au paprika*, Maigret drank *Costières-du-Gard*.

Boeuf en Miroton

(Boiled Beef with Onions)

> The smell coming from the kitchen was exactly
> the same as that of the stew upstairs.
>
> *Les Caves du Majestic*

- Chop 8 large onions. Boil them 1 minute. Drain and wipe.
- Melt 4 Tb. of lard in a heavy saucepan and turn the onions in it
  until they are slightly colored. Add 3 Tb. of flour and, stirring
  constantly with a wooden spoon, brown the onions.
- Add 2 Tb. of vinegar to the onions. Cool.
- Put back on heat and add 2 cups of very hot beef stock (or
  bouillon), stirring well to avoid lumps. Then add 1 tsp. of tomato
  paste, 2 cloves of garlic, and some ground pepper. Simmer for
  20 minutes.
- Cut in thin slices about 1 lb. of beef, previously boiled, and place
  these in an ovenproof dish.
- Remove the boiling sauce from heat and take out the garlic (if it is
  still intact). Pour the sauce over beef slices. Sprinkle with freshly
  cut parsley and dry bread crumbs. Add some melted butter and
  brown in a hot oven for about 15 minutes. Serve.

COURTINE'S NOTE: Spread the flour used in the recipe on a baking
sheet and let it brown in the oven before adding it to the onions.

With the *boeuf en miroton*, Maigret drank *Moulin-à-Vent*.

Huchpot

(*Dutch Stew*)

> *Huchpot*, the national dish, was brought in. The meat
> was literally swimming in the sauce.
>
> *A Crime in Holland*

- Boil slowly 1½ lbs. of plate (or brisket) in 2 qts. of water to which
  has been added 2 carrots, 2 onions each studded with a clove, a
  bouquet garni (see Note, page 15), salt and pepper, for 2½ hours.
- When the meat is half cooked, add 1 lb. of peeled potatoes.
- When the meat has finished cooking, slice it and place it on a hot
  platter. Pour some of the beef bouillon into a saucepan and mash
  the potatoes in it. Add more bouillon until you have a thick sauce
  of mashed potatoes. Taste for seasoning. Pour the sauce over the
  meat and serve.
- Serve with capers, sweet pickles, and pickled onions.

COURTINE'S NOTE: The truth of the matter is that Madame Maigret
prefers to make her *commissaire* husband a Ghent *hochepot* rather than
a Holland *huchpot*. She puts a quartered pig's foot, a pig's ear cut in
squares, an oxtail cut in small pieces, and ¾ lb. of diced breast of veal
in a large pot to which she adds the same vegetables and herbs as above.
Then she puts in a Savoy cabbage cut in quarters. All this she lets
cook for 45 minutes. Then she adds 1 lb. of peeled potatoes cut in
quarters and lets the *hochepot* boil for another 30 minutes.

With the *huchpot*, Maigret drank *Château Pétrus (Pomerol)*.

Boeuf Bourguignon

(*Beef Stew Burgundy Style*)

> Madame Maigret had made a *boeuf bourguignon* as only
> she knew how, and this dish, at once substantial and
> subtle, became the center of conversation.
>
> Then they talked about provincial cooking: *cassoulet,
> potée lorraine, tripes à la mode de Caen.* . . .
>
> "Actually most of these dishes were invented out of
> necessity. If they'd had refrigerators in the
> Middle Ages . . ."
>
> *Maigret and the Killer*

- Make a marinade consisting of 2 small chopped leeks, 2 carrots
  cut in rounds, 2 large coarsely chopped onions, 1 stalk of diced
  celery, 3 cloves of crushed garlic, a *bouquet garni* (use two sprigs
  of fresh parsley, one sprig of thyme, fresh if possible, tied with
  ½ bay leaf), salt and pepper, and a bottle of red Burgundy.
- Cut 1¾ lb. of lean stewing beef into 2-inch pieces. Place in the
  marinade and leave, covered, for 48 hours.
- At the end of this time remove the meat and drain it carefully.
  Strain the marinade.
- Melt 4 Tb. of lard in a Dutch oven. Brown the meat over high heat.
  Add the herbs from the marinade. Sprinkle 2 Tb. of flour that has
  been browned in the oven (see Note, page 94) on the meat.
  Stir the meat with a wooden spatula so that the flour forms a
  crust on each piece.
- Heat the marinade and pour over meat. Add 1 or 2 cups of hot
  water. (The meat should be well covered with liquid.)
- Blanch 5–6 oz. of salt pork and add to the meat. Taste for
  seasoning. Cover and cook gently for 3½ hours.
- Blanch 20 small white pearl onions and add them to the meat.
  Take out the *bouquet garni*. Cook for 15 minutes.
- Remove from fire and add 1 tsp. of *marc de Bourgogne* (brandy).
- Before serving the meat, sprinkle it with freshly cut parsley.

COURTINE'S NOTE: If you would like small mushrooms in this dish, add about 2 cups at the same time as the onions.

A purée of celery root is an agreeable complement to this dish.

With the *boeuf bourguignon*, Maigret drank *Santenay*.

Boeuf Rôti à la Bordelaise

(Roast Beef Bordelaise Style)

"What are you planning for lunch?"

"A roast beef with celery hearts and mashed potatoes."

It reminded him of his childhood. The Sunday roast!
At that time he liked it very well done . . .

Maigret and the Wine Merchant

- Salt and pepper a 2½-lb. sirloin roast and place it in a deep bowl.
  Cover it with sliced onions, chopped shallots, 2 or 3 sprigs of
  parsley, a bay leaf, and some sprigs of thyme (or a pinch of dried
  thyme). Pour 1 cup of dry white wine and 1 cup of olive oil over it.
  Keep it in a cool place overnight.
- Melt a little lard in a roasting pan and add the onion, shallot, and
  herbs from the strained marinade. Place the roast in the pan.
  Heat the marinade and pour about ¼ cup over the roast. Cook
  about 45 minutes in a medium oven, basting frequently with the
  drippings.
- Place the roast on a hot platter. Strain the juice and skim off fat.
  (If there is too much juice, cook it down on top of the stove.)
- Salt the roast lightly, pour a little sauce over it, and serve the rest
  in a sauce boat.

COURTINE'S NOTE: For the garnish, you will need a can containing
4 large celery hearts. Cut them in half lengthwise. Rinse, then wipe
them. Melt some butter in a pan and add the celery hearts sprinkled
with salt and pepper. Cover and steam in the oven for a few minutes.
Pour some of the meat sauce over them and arrange them on a platter
with the roast.

With the *rôti de boeuf à la bordelaise*, Maigret drank *Domaine
de Chevalier (Graves rouge)*.

Côte de Boeuf Braisée

(Braised Rib Roast)

> "They've got *coquilles Saint Jacques*. What do you say?"
> "*Coquilles Saint Jacques* are all right with me. . . ."
> "And how about *côte de boeuf braisée?* . . ."
> "Great!"
>
> *Maigret and the Informer*

- Choose a lean 4–6 lb. rib roast. Lard it with 10 strips of fat trimmed from fresh ham, which have been seasoned with pepper and dried herbs, sprinkled with freshly cut parsley, and soaked an hour in brandy.
- Put the rib roast in a marinade consisting of one bottle of red wine, 2 onions each studded with a clove, 2 carrots cut in rounds, and a *bouquet garni* (see Note, page 15). Turn the meat several times. After 4 hours, remove the meat from the marinade. Drain it and wipe it dry.
- Melt 3 Tb. of lard in a Dutch oven and brown the meat. Add the onions and carrots from the marinade and 2 lbs. of beef bones which have been slightly browned in the oven. Salt and pepper the roast. Pour the marinade over the meat. (If in the course of cooking there does not seem to be enough liquid, add some beef bouillon.) Cover and braise the meat in a slow oven for about 4 hours.
- Place the meat on a hot platter. Strain the juice, skim off fat, and reduce liquid for a few minutes. Taste for seasoning. Serve the sauce separately.

COURTINE'S NOTE: French fried potatoes or souffléed potatoes go well with this dish.

With the *côte de boeuf braisée*, Maigret drank *Château Léoville-Las-Cases*.

Roastbeef Froid Sauce Mousquetaire

(Cold Roast Beef with Sauce Mousquetaire)

> He got home early, ate some cold meat, cheese, and
> salad and devoted the rest of the evening to television.
> *Maigret and the Loner*

> Eating cold meat they watched the sky darken, the streets
> empty, and the houses across the way light up.
> *Maigret Loses His Temper*

- Cut fairly thick slices of cold well-done roast beef and arrange them in overlapping slices on a platter. Place some chopped meat jelly in the center. Serve a *sauce mousquetaire* in a sauce boat.

Sauce Mousquetaire:
- Chop 4 shallots. Put them in a saucepan with ⅓ cup of dry white wine and 1 tsp. of white wine vinegar. Add a generous pinch of pepper. Boil down until very thick.
- With a wooden spatula scrape up the residue from the bottom of the pan. Strain. Place in a clean pan. Add 1 tsp. of beef extract. Cool.
- Make some mayonnaise. Add it to the boiled-down wine sauce along with 1 tsp. of chopped chives.

COURTINE'S NOTE: Madame Maigret makes her mayonnaise with 2 egg yolks, a pinch of salt and another of white pepper, and 1 cup of pure olive oil, first added drop by drop, then teaspoon by teaspoon, to the yolks. If the mayonnaise seems too thick, she adds a fine trickle of vinegar. If it separates, she beats another egg yolk and very slowly adds the separated mayonnaise to it.

With the *roastbeef froid*, Maigret drank *Chinon (Clos de l'Echo)*.

Escalopes à la Florentine

(*Veal Cutlets Florentine Style*)

> "Angelino! Bring these gentlemen the *escalopes à la Florentine*. Tell Giovanni to cook them as if they were for me. I hope you like *escalopes à la Florentine*, *commissaire?*"
>
> *Maigret and the Gangsters*

- Have 1¾ lb. of veal cut into thin cutlets. Salt and pepper them. Turn them in flour.
- Heat 3 Tb. of pure olive oil in a heavy skillet. Brown the cutlets, allowing 2 minutes for each side.
- Place the cutlets on a hot platter. Pour out most of the oil from the skillet and add ⅔ cup of veal bouillon. Bring to a boil, scraping up the coagulated juice with a wooden spatula. Put the cutlets back in the skillet. Cover with 6 slices of lemon. Cover the skillet and simmer for ¼ hour.
- Remove the cutlets and place them on a hot platter.
- Pick over and wash 2 lbs. of spinach. Cook it in a large pot in boiling salted water for 10 minutes.
- Drain the spinach. Rinse it in cold water. Drain it again, then squeeze it with your hands to extract every drop of water. Re-heat in a saucepan with 4 Tb. of butter. Add salt and pepper.
- Reduce the liquid in the skillet used for cooking the cutlets. With the back of a spoon press the juice from the lemon slices. Strain and mix into the spinach.
- Place the spinach on a hot platter, arrange the cutlets on top, and serve.

COURTINE'S NOTE: Occasionally Madame Maigret sprinkles grated Parmesan cheese on top of the dish and browns it a minute in the oven.

Be sure to use lemons untreated with chemical spray.

With the *escalopes à la Florentine*, Maigret drank *Chianti*.

Fricandeau à l'Oseille

(Fricandeau *with Sorrel*)

"You won't find a lot on the menu here. You have to take
the specialty of the day. . . . What do you know!
It's *fricandeau à l'oseille*. . . ."

"One of my favorite dishes . . ."

Les Nouvelles Enquêtes de Maigret

She'd made him one of his favorite dishes, *fricandeau
à l'oseille.*

Maigret and the Madwoman

"Well! Here you are at last, Maigret . . . I was
beginning to wonder. . . . I've made you *fricandeau
à l'oseille* just as you asked me to when you phoned. . . ."

To Any Length

- Heat some olive oil in a heavy casserole until it is almost smoking.
  Brown a 3–3½ lb. rolled veal roast in it. Remove meat.
- Line the bottom of the casserole with cracklings and put the
  meat on top. Add ½ calf's foot, 2 carrots cut in rounds, and an
  onion studded with a clove. Pour in 2 cups of dry white wine and
  2 cups of veal bouillon. Salt lightly and bring to a boil.
- Cook fairly briskly for 40 minutes, then simmer for 1 hour. Just
  before the meat is done, pepper it generously. The sauce will be
  thick and gelatinous.
- Pick over and wash in several waters 1 lb. of spinach. Cook it in a
  large pan full of boiling salted water for about 10 minutes. Drain.
- Pick over and wash in several waters 2 lbs. of sorrel. Drain. Warm
  1 Tb. of olive oil in a large saucepan. Add the sorrel. Stir frequently
  as it cooks in its rendered water. When all the water has evaporated,
  salt it lightly and mix it with the spinach. Add ½ cup of heavy
  cream. Set aside in a warm place.
- Place the veal on a hot platter. Strain the sauce, skim off fat, and
  pour over the meat. Serve the spinach and sorrel in a separate
  vegetable dish.

COURTINE'S NOTE: The veal for this dish should be cut from the leg. If you wish, you may omit the spinach in this recipe. In that case you will need 3 lbs. of sorrel, but preparing the dish as Madame Maigret does, it will have a more delicate consistency.

With the *fricandeau à l'oseille*, Maigret drank *Bordeaux Côtes de Fronsac*.

Blanquette de Veau

(Veal Stew in Cream Sauce)

"How about a bottle of *Bourgueil?* It will be perfect
with the *blanquette.* . . ."

The *blanquette* was just creamy enough, the sauce a
golden yellow and wonderfully fragrant.

Maigret and the Wine Merchant

"What did you make us for dinner?"

"Blanquette de veau."

Maigret and the Madwoman

They served a *blanquette de veau* that Madame Maigret
could not have improved on.

Maigret's Failure

"We have *blanquette de veau,*" the chef announced.

"Will that do?"

"That's fine."

Maigret's Childhood Friend

- Place 2–2½ lbs. of veal stew meat cut into fairly large pieces in a
  bowl of lukewarm water and let it stand for ½ hour. Drain.
- Put the pieces in a large casserole, cover with cold water, add a
  pinch of salt, and bring to a boil. Skim. Add an onion studded with
  2 cloves, 2 carrots cut in rounds, ⅔ cup of dry white wine, and a
  bouquet garni (see Note, page 15). Simmer for ¾ hour. Take the
  meat out and drain it. Wash casserole and return meat to it.
- Melt 4 Tb. of butter in a large heavy saucepan and blend in 2 Tb.
  of flour. Add the strained veal stock and cook very slowly, stirring
  with a wooden spoon until the stock is thick and smooth. Add
  pepper.
- Pour stock over the veal pieces in the casserole and cook slowly
  for 30 minutes, or until the sauce is reduced by half. Remove
  from fire.

- Using a fork beat 2 egg yolks into ½ cup of heavy cream. Add the juice of 1 lemon. Add this mixture little by little to the meat and sauce. Then heat very slowly for about 5 minutes, taking care it does not boil. Taste for seasoning.
- Place the *blanquette* in a hot serving dish and sprinkle with freshly cut parsley. Garnish with croûtons sautéed in butter.

COURTINE'S NOTE: A mint leaf added to the *bouquet garni* gives the sauce an interesting taste—and fragrance. Serve long-grain American rice with the *blanquette*.

With the *blanquette de veau*, Maigret drank *Château Magence* (*Graves blanc*), or a young *Bourgueil*.

Rouelle de Veau aux Lentilles

(Rolled Veal with Lentils)

> The menu was written in chalk on a slate:
> *Rillettes du Morvan*
> *Rouelle de veau aux lentilles*
> Cheese
> *Tarte* made by the chef . . .
> "D'you like *rouelle?*" Maigret muttered.
> "I like all the local dishes. I'm a farmer's son myself, and my brother runs the family farm."
>
> *The Patience of Maigret*

- Pick over and wash 2 cups of lentils. Cover them with warm water and soak for 2 hours.
- Drain the lentils. Put them in 13 cups of cold water to which has been added 3 Tb. of salt and ¼ tsp. of baking soda. Bring them to a boil very slowly (this should take about ½ hour).
- When the water boils, skim it and add a generous *bouquet garni* (consisting of thyme, parsley, bay leaf), a stalk of celery, 2 onions each studded with a clove, and 1 clove of garlic. Boil very gently for 1½ hours.
- Melt 2 Tb. of lard in a casserole, add a 3–3½ lb. rolled veal roast and brown it.
- Cut a carrot in rounds, chop 3 shallots coarsely, and arrange around meat. Salt and pepper the meat. Add 2 cups of veal bouillon and cook gently for about 1 hour.
- Drain the lentils. Add them to the casserole containing the meat, and cook for another 15 minutes. Add 1 Tb. of butter and serve.

COURTINE'S NOTE: It goes without saying that you will use "green" lentils from Puy. And this year's crop!

With the *rouelle de veau aux lentilles*, Maigret drank *Châteaugay*.

Épaule de Mouton Farcie Bonne Femme

(Stuffed Shoulder of Mutton)

> The main dish was *épaule de mouton farcie*. Maigret
> couldn't recall ever having eaten anything like it.
>
> *Maigret Afraid*

> They left the Pardons around eleven after their usual
> monthly dinner, consisting this time of a succulent
> *épaule de mouton farcie*.
>
> *Maigret and the Nahour Case*

- In a deep bowl knead thoroughly 8–10 oz. of sausage meat with 2 small- or 1 medium-sized chopped onions (cooked in butter until just barely colored), 3 slices of stale bread that have been soaked a moment in bouillon then squeezed out, 2 tsp. freshly chopped parsley, and 1 lightly beaten egg. Taste for seasoning, which should be strong.
- Spread the stuffing on a 2½ lb. boned shoulder of mutton (or lamb). Roll it up lengthwise and tie it (see Note).
- Melt 1 Tb. of lard in a Dutch oven. Add the meat. Spread 1 Tb. of lard on top of the meat and brown it thoroughly on all sides. Cover and place in a moderate oven for 1 hour, turning it 3 or 4 times in the course of cooking.
- Scrape 6 carrots, cut them in quarters, and place them in 3 quarts of unsalted boiling water. Cook for 15 minutes. Add 1 lb. of fresh string beans. Cook another 15 minutes. Drain.
- Heat some butter in a skillet and brown 2 thinly sliced onions.
- Arrange the carrots and string beans around the stuffed shoulder. Place the browned onions on top. Cover and bake for ½ hour, basting from time to time with the cooking juices. Taste for seasoning before serving.

COURTINE'S NOTE: Tie the meat firmly lengthwise and crosswise so the string will not loosen too much as the meat shrinks in cooking.

With the *épaule de mouton farcie*, Maigret drank *Cahors*.

Haricot de Mouton

(*Mutton Stew*)

> "Is that you, Madame Maigret?" he said jokingly to his
> wife when he had her on the line. "I won't be home for
> lunch. What's your menu?"
>
> "*Haricot de mouton.*"
>
> He wasn't too sorry. It would have been too heavy
> for a day like this.
>
> *Maigret and the Headless Corpse*

- Cut 2½ lbs. of breast of mutton (or lamb) into 1½-inch pieces.
- Melt a little lard in a heavy casserole and brown 4 ounces of lean
  bacon strips (previously simmered for 10 minutes). Add the meat
  and brown on all sides.
- Remove all fat from the pan. Sprinkle the meat with flour. Turn
  and stir the meat with a wooden spatula until the flour has formed
  a crust. Add ⅔ cup of dry white wine and enough bouillon to cover.
  Add a *bouquet garni* (see Note, page 15). Cover and simmer
  for 1 hour.
- Remove the meat and strips of bacon. Strain the juice and skim
  off the fat.
- Peel 1¼ lbs. of spring turnips. Wipe (rather than wash) them
  thoroughly.
- Clean the casserole in which the meat was cooked with paper
  toweling and add the meat and strained juice. Bring to a boil.
  Taste for seasoning. Add the turnips, cover, and cook for 1 hour
  in a moderate oven.

COURTINE'S NOTE: The word *haricot* (bean) is a deformation of the
word *halicot*, which comes from an Old French verb *halicoter*, meaning
to cut in thin slices. In other words, there are no beans in *haricot de
mouton*. This dish was known long before the discovery of America
which brought beans to Europe.

With the *haricot de mouton*, Maigret drank *Chinon*.

Ragoût de Mouton

(Mutton Stew)

> It seemed to him that his throat was still coated with the
> fat from the *ragoût de mouton* he had eaten at the
> Auvergnat's house, which had seemed so succulent
> to him at the time.
>
> *Maigret Takes a Room*

- Cut 2½ lbs. of boned shoulder of lamb into 1½-inch pieces. Season with salt, pepper, and nutmeg.
- Heat 2 Tb. of lard in an enameled iron casserole, add the meat and brown it on all sides, using a wooden spoon for turning. Take out the meat pieces and set them in a sieve over a bowl. Empty the casserole and wipe it with paper toweling.
- Melt 2 Tb. of butter in the casserole. Add 3 Tb. of flour, and blend butter and flour over a low flame until smooth and golden. Stirring rapidly, add 2 cups of bouillon. Continue stirring until the sauce boils.
- Add the pieces of meat and the bowl of rendered juice. If the meat is not completely covered with liquid, add more bouillon.
- Add 1 lb. of peeled and seeded tomatoes cut in chunks, a *bouquet garni* (see Note, page 15), and a large onion studded with 2 cloves. Simmer, covered, for 1 hour on very low heat.
- Place the meat on a hot platter. Strain the juice. Wash and dry the casserole.
- Put the meat and juice back in the casserole. Add about 20 small white peeled pearl onions, about 2 lbs. of potatoes peeled and cut in quarters, and some salt and pepper. Cover and cook for 1 hour in a moderate oven.

COURTINE'S NOTE: You can make your own bouillon for this dish using the bones and meat trimmings your butcher has cut from the shoulder.

With the *ragoût de mouton*, Maigret drank *Châteauneuf-du-Pape*.

Navarin Printanier

(Lamb Stew with Spring Vegetables)

> The restaurant was very old-fashioned. The specialty
> of the day was written on a slate: *navarin printanier.*
>
> *Félicie est là*

- Cut about 2½ lbs. of boned shoulder of lamb into 1–2-inch pieces. Salt and pepper them.
- Place 6 Tb. of lard in a casserole and, when it is smoking hot, add the meat pieces. Sprinkle them with a good pinch of sugar and, stirring with a wooden spoon, brown the meat on all sides.
- Spoon out three-quarters of the fat. Add ⅓ cup of flour. Stir and turn the meat until the flour has formed a crust on the meat. Add 6½ cups of bouillon. Bring to a boil, stirring and scraping up from the bottom with a wooden spatula. Add salt and pepper. Add 4 very ripe peeled tomatoes, a clove of crushed garlic, and a *bouquet garni* (see Note, page 15). Cover and simmer for 1¼ hours.
- Discard the *bouquet garni.* Take out the meat pieces and put them in a bowl. Skim the fat off the juice and pour it over the meat. Wash and dry the casserole.
- Put the meat and juice back in the casserole and place over a medium fire. When the juice begins to boil gently and regularly, add 6 spring turnips trimmed into ovals and 6 carrots (which have all been heated a few minutes in a little hot lard). Cover and continue to boil gently for 20 minutes.
- Add a scant lb. of scraped new potatoes, about 20 small white pearl onions, a cup of fresh green peas, and 1½ cups of French-cut string beans. Make sure that all the vegetables are well-covered by the sauce. Taste for seasoning. Turn down heat and simmer for ¾ hour.

COURTINE'S NOTE: After adding the flour to the meat, remember to stir well so that the flour doesn't stick to the bottom of the casserole. To remove the fat, tilt the pan and with a spoon skim off the fat that rises to the surface. Wipe rather than wash the turnips and carrots before placing them in the hot lard. This will seal their color. If necessary, skim the fat off the sauce again before serving.

With the *navarin printanier*, Maigret drank *Pomerol*.

Gigot à la Bretonne

(Leg of Lamb Breton Style)

> The *gigot* was done to a turn and the beans melted in your
> mouth. The doctor had brought out a bottle of old wine.
>
> *Maigret Goes to School*

- Put 1½ lbs. of dry white beans in an earthenware pot. Cover with
  2 qts. of water, add a pinch of baking soda, and slowly bring to a
  boil. Remove from heat and let stand for 1 hour. Drain.
- Put the beans back in the pot. Cover with 2 qts. of boiling water.
  Add salt, an onion studded with a clove, 2 cloves of crushed garlic,
  and a *bouquet garni* (see Note, page 15). Simmer for 1½ hours.
  Set aside (in the cooking water).
- Rub a 5–6 lb. leg of lamb with garlic, then with lard. Roast it in a
  preheated moderate oven (see Note). Baste it from time to time
  with melted lard.
- Chop an onion and cook it a moment in lard. Sprinkle it with flour
  and brown. Add ½ cup of dry white wine and ¼ cup of bouillon,
  stirring well. Add 4 Tb. of tomato paste, salt and pepper.
  Cook slowly about 10 minutes.
- Drain the beans (heating first if necessary). Put them in a
  vegetable dish and mix in the sauce.
- Place the leg of lamb on a hot platter and its juice in a sauce boat.

COURTINE'S NOTE: For the lamb, allow 15 minutes roasting time for
the first pound, and 12 minutes for each additional pound.

With the *gigot à la bretonne*, Maigret drank *Rouge de l'Île de Ré*.

Gigot d'Agneau à la Provençale

(Leg of Lamb Provence Style)

> He ate heartily. The *gigot* was a delicate pink with the
> barest trickle of blood next to the bone: "Marvelous,"
> he sighed, helping himself to another slice.
>
> *Maigret and the Loner*

- Remove loose fat from a small leg of lamb (2½–3½ lbs.).
- Rub a deep baking dish with garlic, then butter it.
- Peel 1½–2 lbs. of potatoes, cut them in thick slices, and arrange
  in layers in the dish. Sprinkle salt, pepper, freshly cut parsley, and
  a little crushed garlic on top of each layer. Place the leg of
  lamb on top.
- Moisten with chicken consommé. Bake in a moderate oven for about
  1 hour. (Test potatoes for doneness.) Serve in the same
  baking dish.

COURTINE'S NOTE: There are two ways of carving a leg of lamb—
either parallel to the bone or perpendicular to the bone. In the first,
the blood stays in and the slices are uniformly done. In the second, the
slices are more rare at the bone end.

With the *gigot d'agneau à la provençale*, Maigret drank *Rouge
de Bellet*.

Gigot d'Agneau en Gelée

(Leg of Lamb in Aspic)

Maigret looked at the pink flesh of the *gigot*, and what
was left of the tasty salad. It was really tempting. . . .

He was hungry. And there was the *gigot* almost under
his nose. There were two slices on the platter. He picked
them up in his hand, ate them, and went on talking,
as if he were one of the family.

Liberty Bar

- Select a leg of lamb that, when trimmed, does not weigh more than
  4½ lbs. Pound it.
- Cover the bottom of an open pan with a very thin layer of
  chopped garlic.
- Coat the lamb with olive oil, then with a thin layer of salt butter.
  Put it in the pan and roast at 325° for 1 hour (or more if you prefer
  it well done—Tr.).
- When the lamb is cooked, place it in a deep mold or baking dish.
  Pour strained jellied stock over it (you can use a commercial
  product—Tr.), and set it in a cool place.
- Unmold the lamb after 12 hours. Serve it with lettuce salad.

COURTINE'S NOTE: Pound the lamb with a rolling pin. This softens
the skin and makes the meat more tender.

With the *gigot d'agneau en gelée*, Maigret drank a young *Fleurie*.

Côtelettes d'Agneau au Romarin

(*Lamb Chops with Rosemary*)

> After the sweetbreads, which were delicious, they had
> tiny lamb chops, and for dessert a strawberry tart.
>
> *Maigret and the Madwoman*

- Allow 2 thick rib lamb chops per person.
- Put 2 Tb. of pure olive oil, a pinch of salt, and ½ tsp. of rosemary in a bowl. Mix well.
- Brush the chops with this fragrant mixture.
- Broil 3 minutes on each side (or a little more if you like it well done—Tr.). Serve.

COURTINE'S NOTE: The perfect accompaniment to the broiled chops is watercress salad with olive oil and mustard dressing.

With the *côtelettes d'agneau*, Maigret drank *Château de Selle rouge*.

Rôti de Porc aux Lentilles

(*Roast Pork with Lentils*)

"Can we eat here?"

"Of course you can . . . What would you like?
Fricandeau with sorrel? . . . Roast pork with lentils?
. . . We have a good *pâté de campagne* as a starter."

The Most Obstinate Man in Paris

- Prepare the following cooked marinade: mince 3 carrots, 3 onions,
  2 shallots, and a stalk of celery, and sauté lightly in olive oil.
  Add a sprig of thyme, a bay leaf, and some parsley. When the
  vegetables are slightly soft, add 1 bottle of dry white wine along
  with 6 peppercorns and 2 cloves. Boil for 10 minutes.
  Set aside to cool.
- Choose a loin or shoulder roast of pork weighing about 3 lbs.
  Cut off loose bits of fat if necessary. Place in the cooled marinade
  for several hours. Remove meat and drain.
- Preheat oven and regulate it to moderate (325°–350°). Place the
  roast on the rack over the roasting pan, fatty side up. Bake,
  allowing 30 minutes to the pound.
- When the fat is nicely browned, baste the roast with a little warm
  water. For testing doneness, pierce the roast deeply with a knitting
  needle. The juice that appears should be a clear yellow.
- While the meat is roasting, cook a package (about 2 cups) of
  lentils (previously soaked for an hour) in salted water to which a
  pinch of soda, an onion studded with a clove, a carrot cut in rounds,
  and a *bouquet garni* (see Note, page 15) have been added.
  When the lentils are done, drain them and discard the
  bouquet garni.
- Remove meat from oven and pour the juice into a bowl. Cool the
  juice and skim off the fat. Place the roasting pan on the fire, add a
  bit of the marinade, and scrape the coagulated juice up from the
  bottom with a wooden spatula. Mix this in with the degreased meat
  juice and season the lentils with it. Add a Tb. of butter and place
  the lentils in a serving dish. Sprinkle with freshly cut parsley
  and serve with the roast.

COURTINE'S NOTE: I find loin pork or filet of pork too dry for this dish. Ask your butcher for shoulder or blade end.

Here is Madame Maigret's alternate recipe for a marinade for roast pork. Boil 5 sage leaves (or a pinch of dried sage) in 4 cups of water. Add 2 cups of dry white wine, 5 cloves of garlic, and 5 peppercorns. Before placing the pork roast in the marinade, rub it with coarse salt.

With the *rôti de porc aux lentilles*, Maigret drank *Corent*.

Côte de Porc Farcie

(Stuffed Pork Chop)

> "Soup, fish, and a pork chop with cabbage . . ."
>
> *La Maison du Juge*

- Prepare 2 thick pork chops for stuffing: trim off excess fat. With the sharp point of a knife make a 2-inch slit in the narrow side of each chop. Rotate the knife so as to enlarge the pocket—until the knife touches the bone opposite the slit.
- Dice 4 slices of salami. Cut ¼ lb. of Emmenthaler or Gruyère cheese into thin slices. Mix these with salt, pepper, some freshly cut parsley, and a sage leaf (or a pinch of dried sage).
- Stuff the chops with this mixture, pressing it in firmly.
- Melt some lard in a heavy skillet and sauté chops until brown. Salt the chops, place them in a baking dish, cover, and cook in a preheated oven (325°) for 25 to 30 minutes.
- Serve with cabbage purée.

COURTINE'S NOTE: Cook the cabbage in two waters. Peel and cook 2 potatoes. Put potatoes and cabbage through a vegetable mill. Place the purée in a hot oven for a few minutes to get rid of excess moisture. Dot with butter and serve.

With the *côte de porc farcie aux choux*, Maigret drank young *Chiroubles*.

Cassoulet

(*Stew of Goose, Pork, and Sausage*)

"What is there for supper?"
"The warmed-over lunch."
"And what was there for lunch?"
"*Cassoulet.*"

Maigret Hesitates

- Soak 2 lbs. of dry white beans (be sure they're not stale) overnight.
  Drain and place them in a large bowl of unsalted cold water.
  Add a pinch of baking soda. Bring to a boil, skim, and lower heat.
- Mince a carrot, an onion, and a clove of garlic, and brown in
  goosefat. Add to the beans. Add a *bouquet garni* (see Note,
  page 15). Simmer for ½ hour. Discard *bouquet garni*.
- In a heavy skillet, brown pieces (about 2 lbs.) of preserved goose
  (*confit d'oie*) with all the fat removed (if *confit d'oie* cannot be
  found, pieces of roasted goose, duck, or turkey may be substituted—Tr.). At the same time, brown 6 slices of cooked loin of
  pork and about ¾ lb. of Polish sausage. Add these to the beans.
  Continue slow cooking.
- When the skins of the beans start to burst, pour the contents of
  the pan into a deep earthenware casserole. Bake in a slow
  oven for 1 hour.
- Set aside to cool, preferably overnight. Before reheating (in a
  slow oven), break the top crust and mix it into the other
  ingredients. Add a little water and reheat slowly.

COURTINE'S NOTE: Some people add tomato paste to the cassoulet, but
it is really not advisable.

With the *cassoulet*, Maigret drank *Villaudric*.

Choucroute à l'Alsacienne

(Alsatian Sauerkraut)

The waitress was wearing an Alsatian costume. He was glad to see that she looked sturdy and healthy. With her smile and dimples and curly blond hair she seemed so devoid of psychological complications that he found it perfectly natural to order one of those lavish *choucroutes* with glistening sausages and blushingly pink *petit salé*.

Maigret and the Reluctant Witnesses

Twenty minutes later, Maigret, seated across from his wife, was relishing a savory *choucroute à l'alsacienne*—the kind you find in only two restaurants in Paris. The *petit salé* was particularly tasty and the *commissaire* had opened two bottles of Strasbourg beer.

Maigret and the Nahour Case

- Melt ½ cup of goosefat (4 oz.) in a large flameproof casserole and add a minced onion. Place on top a layer of thinly sliced apples.
- Wash 4 lbs. of raw sauerkraut. Place one-third of this in the bottom of the casserole. Tie 5 peppercorns and 5 juniper berries loosely in cheesecloth and place on top of the sauerkraut. Add another layer of sauerkraut, another cheesecloth bag containing 5 peppercorns and 5 juniper berries, and end with a top layer of sauerkraut. Dot this with 3 Tb. of fresh rendered goosefat. Add 2 cups of water and 2 cups of dry white wine (Alsatian wine, if possible). Cover, place on a low fire, and cook for 1 hour.

- After this hour of cooking, stir the sauerkraut thoroughly and take out half. On the remaining half place ¾ lb. of fat salt pork, ¾ lb. of bacon (in a chunk), a small ham butt, the leg of a smoked goose, and ¾ lb. of *petit salé** (previously soaked for 1 hour in cold water). Cover with the rest of the sauerkraut. Cook in a moderate oven, covered, for 1½ hours.
- Ten minutes before removing sauerkraut from oven, place 8 frank-furters (or small smoked sausage links) in a pan of boiling water. Turn heat low, simmer for about 8 minutes without ever allowing the water to boil.
- After removing the bags of peppercorns and juniper berries,† turn the sauerkraut and meat onto a large hot platter. Surround it with the frankfurters. Serve a big bowl of steamed potatoes with this dish.

COURTINE'S NOTE: Add a glass of white wine cut with warm water if the sauerkraut has soaked up all the liquid at any point in its cooking.

With the *choucroute à l'alsacienne*, Maigret drank beer.

* *Petit salé:* various cuts of pork (*i.e.* chine, plate) which have been salted down, in other words, corned, as in corned beef. It must be washed carefully—sometimes soaked—to remove its salt. It looks like a gray lump when purchased, but turns a succulent dark-rose color as it cooks. If you cannot find any *petit salé* for your sauerkraut, you can use a piece of corned beef in its place (but don't tell Monsieur Courtine).   Tr.

† If juniper berries are unavailable, use instead 1 jigger of gin.

Choucroute du Pays

(Sauerkraut Country Style)

- Wash 3½ lbs. of raw sauerkraut in cold water. Squeeze the water out. Wash again in hot water. Drain, squeezing with the hands.
- Melt some lard in the bottom of a casserole. Add a layer of thinly sliced apples. Place the sauerkraut on top, and in this bury a cheesecloth bag containing 1 clove of garlic and 6 juniper berries (see foonote, page 121). Pour in enough dry white wine mixed with water to half cover the sauerkraut (use Alsatian wine, if possible). Add 5 Tb. of lard and a good pinch of salt. Cover the pan with a round of greased wax paper, place the lid on top, and simmer for 1 hour.
- Stir the sauerkraut thoroughly and add a ¾ lb. chunk of Canadian bacon (or smoked pork chops) and about 1½ lbs. of *petit salé* (see note on *petit salé*, page 121). Cover and cook over low heat for 2 hours. Make sure there is always enough liquid (wine-and-water mixture) in the casserole.
- Peel about 10 good quality boiling potatoes that keep their shape. Place them on top of the sauerkraut so they cook in the steam (about ½ hour).
- Remove the meats and potatoes and arrange them around a hot platter. Drain the sauerkraut and set it in the middle.
- Decorate the platter with a few poached frankfurters and some liver dumplings.

COURTINE'S NOTE: Here is a recipe for liver dumplings: grind coarsely
1 lb. of pork shoulder, ½ lb. of pork liver, 1 onion, 3 cloves of garlic,
1 white part of a leek, and a few sprigs of parsley. Bind these together
with 2 eggs. Add 1 cup of flour and some salt and pepper. Mix well.
Form into balls the size of a small egg and drop them in boiling salted
water. When they rise to the surface, fish them out with a skimmer.

With the *choucroute du pays*, Maigret drank Alsatian *Pinot rouge*.

Choucroute à la Parisienne

(Sauerkraut Paris Style)

All of a sudden he felt like taking his American to a
brasserie in Montmartre or Montparnasse for a
choucroute garnie.

Cécile est morte

"What about a bite to eat?" he suggested.

"There's a brasserie down the street and I promise you
one of those *choucroutes garnies.* . . ."

. . . He ordered a second portion of *choucroute* with
two frankfurters and a third beer.

Les Nouvelles Enquêtes de Maigret

At a time like this Maigret was a strange mixture of
crude sensual pleasure, voluptuous indulgence of the
flesh, and intense cerebral activity. . . . The two men
had just consumed large bowls of *soupe à l'oignon
gratinée*, and already the waiter was setting lavish
portions of *choucroute garnie* and draft beer before
them. . . .

To Any Length

- Wash and squeeze out the water from 4 lbs. of raw sauerkraut and
  spread out on a towel. Salt it lightly, then sprinkle with pepper and
  nutmeg. Mix with the hands.
- Line the bottom of a large casserole with several slices of clove-
  studded bacon (previously simmered for 10 minutes). On this
  place ⅓ of the sauerkraut. Add 3 whole carrots, 2 onions, a
  bouquet garni (see Note, page 15), and a clove of garlic. Add
  another third of the sauerkraut, 2 more carrots, and 15 juniper
  berries (see footnote, page 121) tied loosely in cheesecloth.
  Top with the rest of the sauerkraut.

- Bury in the sauerkraut a ham butt or hock, a ¾-lb. chunk of bacon (previously simmered for 20 minutes), a ¾-lb. piece of *petit salé* (see Note on *petit salé*, page 121), and a piece of Polish sausage. Cover all this with ⅔ cup of melted lard. Add ⅔ cup of dry white wine, then water until the sauerkraut is about three-quarters covered. Bring to a boil.
- Place in a slow oven and cook, covered, for 3 hours. Remove each piece of meat as it is done and set in a warm place.
- Cook 2 lbs. of firm boiling potatoes in their jackets. Peel them and keep them warm over hot water. Just before the sauerkraut is done poach 6 smoked pork links for about 8 minutes.
- Pile the sauerkraut in the middle of a hot platter. Surround it with the meats and the carrots. Serve the potatoes separately.

COURTINE'S NOTE: Choose your sauerkraut very carefully. If you are not sure about it, let a salesman you know and trust choose it for you.

With the *choucroute à la parisienne*, Maigret drank draft beer.

Potée Lorraine

"No—no sauerkraut—but I wouldn't mind a
potée Lorraine."

Madame Maigret's Own Case

- Put about 3 qts. of water in a large cooking pot, preferably an earthenware *marmite*. Add 2 Tb. of salt, 1 onion studded with 3 cloves, 4 leeks tied up in a bundle, a *bouquet garni* consisting of 2 sprigs of parsley, a celery leaf, a clove of garlic, and a few sprigs of chervil. For coloring, add a handful of pea pods that have been dried in the oven. Bring to a boil.
- Add 4 quartered carrots, 4 sliced turnips, ½ lb. of fresh string beans, and ½ lb. of fresh green peas, including the pods. Simmer for 2 hours. Remove the *bouquet garni* and the pea pods.
- Cut a trimmed cabbage in quarters, blanch it, and add to the *potée*. Boil up the water and add a smoked shoulder of ham. Bring to a boil again and cook slowly for 1½ hours.
- Add a good chunk of lean bacon and a piece of Polish sausage. Bring to a boil. Cook slowly ½ hour.
- Add 5 or 6 potatoes, each sprinkled with salt, to the *potée* water (which by this time should be almost evaporated). Cover and cook until potatoes are done. Place meat and vegetables on a hot platter and serve.

COURTINE'S NOTE: Do not stir the *potée* while it is cooking. Remove the vegetables from the pot with a skimmer; having been cooked so long, they will be quite crushed. The crushed vegetables are a characteristic of this dish. Madame Maigret sometimes puts the vegetables through a vegetable mill and serves them as a purée with the meat.

With the *potée Lorraine*, Maigret drank *Vin gris de Toul*.

Some Vegetables,
a Dish of Mushrooms,
and a
Bowl of Spaghetti

Asperges à la Fontanelle

(*Asparagus with Butter, Cream, and Eggs*)

> They began with asparagus. Afterward they were
> served *raie au beurre noir*.
>
> *Maigret in Society*

- Peel 2 lbs of white asparagus.* Wash carefully, cut to a uniform length, and tie in a bundle.
- Place upright in a deep, narrow pot almost entirely filled with water. Bring to a boil and cook uncovered for from 12 to 15 minutes (or until the stalks are tender).
- Drain, remove strings, and wrap the asparagus in a towel to keep it warm.
- Prepare soft-boiled eggs (allowing 2 per person).
- Melt some butter (about 2 Tb. per person) and place in small cups. Place the same quantity of heavy cream† in other small cups. Arrange the asparagus on a platter.
- Eat the soft-boiled eggs along with the asparagus, and dip each piece of asparagus first in butter, then in cream.

COURTINE'S NOTE: White asparagus is always peeled, never scraped.

With the *asperges à la Fontanelle*, Maigret drank *Blanc de l'île de Ré*.

* Green asparagus can be used if white is unobtainable. It does not have to be peeled.   Tr.

† The French recipe calls for *crème fraîche*, which is much thicker than heavy cream. An approximation can be achieved by combining ⅔ cup of whipping cream with ⅓ cup commercial sour cream. Let mixture thicken 6 hours at room temperature.

Cèpes au Four*

(*Baked Mushrooms*)

> For a moment Maigret thought of the *cèpes* simmering
> on the stove, giving off their aromas of garlic and damp
> woods. He loved *cèpes*.
>
> *Félicie est là*

- Carefully wipe 2 lbs. of large, firm *cèpes* with a damp towel.
  Cut off the stems.
- Heat some pure olive oil in a heavy skillet. When it is almost
  smoking hot, quickly brown the *cèpes*, previously salted and
  peppered. Drain them.
- Place the *cèpes* on a baking sheet, the slightly hollowed-out cut
  ends facing upward. Fill the hollow of each *cèpe* with a mixture of
  breadcrumbs and finely minced garlic. Trickle a bit of olive oil
  over each *cèpe*. Bake for 10 minutes in a hot oven.

COURTINE'S NOTE: Choose *cèpes* of equal size. Make sure they are
fresh and intact.

With the *cèpes au four*, Maigret drank *Château Giscours*.

* *Cèpes*—a fragrant mushroom (*Boletus edulis*). Unhappily, it is obtainable only
in Europe, especially France and Germany. It can be bought canned or dried
in the U.S.   Tr.

Salade de Pommes de Terre

(Potato Salad)

"What would you like to eat?"

"Ham, potatoes in oil, and a green salad. . . ."

Maigret and the Informer

- Peel, wash, then dry 4½ lbs. of firm boiling potatoes. Cut them in cubes.
- Put the potatoes in a large pot of boiling, salted water. Cover and cook for about 12 minutes.
- Make a dressing consisting of 1⅔ cups of pure olive oil, ⅔ cup of dry white wine, 1 tsp. of prepared mustard, salt, and freshly ground pepper.
- Drain the potatoes and place them in a bowl. Pour on the dressing, mix well, sprinkle with freshly cut chives, and serve.

COURTINE'S NOTE: The successfulness of this salad depends on adding the dressing while the potatoes are still warm.

With the *salade de pommes de terre*, Maigret drank *Beaujolais-Villages*.

Pommes de Terre Frites

(French Fried Potatoes)

> Maigret couldn't wait to put the wonderfully crisp
> *pommes frites* in his mouth. Nothing could stop him
> from savoring these really sensational potatoes, crisp on
> the outside, melting soft within.
>
> *Les Caves du Majestic*

> . . . while savoring the crisp and juicy *andouillette*
> served with *pommes frites* that didn't taste of burned fat.
>
> *Maigret Hesitates*

- Wash, peel, wash once more, then wipe large *baking* potatoes.
  Cut in slices about ⅓ inch thick. Then cut into sticks. The future
  French fries should not be more than ⅓ inch wide (preferably
  a bit less). Dry them again in a towel.
- Put a good quantity of peanut oil in a deep-fat frying pan (equipped
  with a frying basket). Heat the oil until it begins to smoke (350°).
  Put some of the potato sticks into the frying basket (without
  crowding) and plunge them into the oil. The cold mass of potatoes
  will cause the temperature to drop to about 320°. When the
  potatoes begin to color, regulate the temperature of the oil to
  about 300°. Fry for five minutes. Remove from basket. Repeat
  this operation until all the potatoes have been cooked once.
- Heat oil again to 350°. Plunge all the potatoes into the oil (in the
  basket, of course). When they are golden brown, remove and
  drain them. Sprinkle with salt and shake them. Place a napkin on a
  platter and arrange the potatoes in a mound.

COURTINE'S NOTE: In place of cooking oil, clarified veal fat can be
used. But whatever kind of fat is employed, it should be used
exclusively for potatoes and other vegetables (or vegetable fritters)
since it will absorb the smell of whatever is fried in it. Do not keep
the fat too long: it will get rancid.

With the *frites*, Maigret drank *Beaujolais* or beer, depending
on the accompaniment.

Spaghetti alla Carbonara

"Two spaghetti for a starter."

"What kind of wine?"

"A fiasco of *Chianti*."

Maigret and the Gangsters

- Place 4 Tb. of butter in a bowl and beat until foamy with a wooden spoon.
- In another bowl beat 2 whole eggs and 2 egg yolks with ⅔ cup of grated Parmesan cheese.
- Put 1 lb. of spaghetti in a large pot of boiling salted water. When the water boils again, cook the spaghetti for about 8 minutes, stirring occasionally with a fork.
- Brown ¼ lb. of lean bacon cut into small pieces in a little butter. Pour off the fat. Then add a small dried hot pepper cut in tiny pieces and ½ cup of heavy cream. Keep in a warm place.
- Drain the spaghetti. Place in a hot bowl. Mix in the foamy butter using two wooden forks. Add the bacon-cream-and-pepper mixture, and finally the eggs and cheese, mixing carefully and quickly.
- Serve the spaghetti as soon as it is impregnated with the sauce and the eggs are cooked (which they will be as soon as they come into contact with the hot spaghetti). Before serving, taste for seasoning and pepper generously.

COURTINE'S NOTE: Spaghetti should be served "al dente," that is, while still slightly resistant to the teeth, not soft and mushy. If you prefer it softer, increase the cooking time.

With the *spaghetti alla carbonara*, Maigret drank *Chianti*.

Desserts

Tarte aux Pommes Bas-Rhinoise

(Apple Tart Rhenish Style)

> A homemade *tarte aux pommes* was served. The smell of
> coffee drifted in from the kitchen.
>
> *Maigret Goes to School*

- Quickly mix together ½ cup of softened butter, 1½ cups of
  all-purpose flour, and ⅓ cup of cornstarch. Add a pinch of salt,
  ¼ cup of sugar, and 1 beaten egg.
- Roll out the dough and place in a large French-style tart pan.*
  Prick the bottom of the pastry with a fork.
- Peel 2 lbs. of cooking apples. Cut them in quarter slices and arrange
  them on the tart dough in concentric circles. Bake in a hot (375°)
  oven for 20 minutes.
- Mix 1⅔ cups of milk with ½ cup of sugar. Stir in 3 Tb. of flour
  and 1 Tb. of cornstarch. Add 1 whole egg and 2 egg yolks.
  Add a little nutmeg. Beat lightly.
- Pour this custard over the tart as soon as it has been removed
  from the oven. Bake for 15 minutes more, or until set.
- Cool tart, sprinkle with powdered sugar, and remove from mold.

COURTINE'S NOTE: Good, crisp, tart cooking apples should be
used for this dish.

With the *tarte aux pommes*, Maigret drank *Tokay d'Alsace*.

* A French-style *tarte* pan consists of a straight-sided metal ring which fits on a
round metal bottom. This makes the *tarte* easy to unmold.   Tr.

Tarte aux Abricots à la Crème Frangipane

(*Apricot Tart with Almond Custard*)

- Make a *pâte brisée* with 2½ cups of flour, ½ cup of softened butter, 1 tsp. of salt, and 6 Tb. of water. Form the dough into a ball, wrap in wax paper, and set in a cool place for several hours.
- Mix ½ cup of sifted all-purpose flour, ½ cup of sugar, a pinch of salt, 1 whole egg, and 4 egg yolks. Stir for 5 minutes. Add 2 cups of milk that has been boiled with a vanilla bean and cooled.
- Bring this mixture slowly to a boil, then cook for 2 minutes, stirring constantly. Remove from fire.
- Add 4 Tb. of melted butter and 2 Tb. of powdered almonds to the custard. Mix well. Place in a bowl to cool.
- Cut in half and remove stones from 2 lbs. of ripe apricots. Poach them for a few minutes in a syrup consisting of ½ cup of water and ½ cup of sugar. Drain them.
- Roll out the dough and place it in a buttered French-style tart pan (see Note, page 137, for a description of this—Tr.). Prick the pastry with a fork. Cover the dough with a round of wax paper and on this place a few pebbles or dry white beans to prevent the dough from puffing. Bake in a hot oven for 20 minutes.
- Remove paper and pebbles (or beans) from the baked crust. Pour in the almond custard, smoothing the surface with the back of a tablespoon. Arrange the apricot halves on the custard. Sprinkle with sugar and serve.

COURTINE'S NOTE: To keep the almond custard from forming a crust, spear a piece of butter on a knife and pass it over the surface while it is still hot.

You might add 1 Tb. of apricot brandy to the sugar syrup in which the apricots are poached.

With the *tarte à la frangipane*, Maigret drank *Mumm cuvée René Lalou.*

Tarte aux Mirabelles

(Yellow Plum Tart)

> It was a juicy *tarte aux prunes* (plums), flavored
> with cinnamon.
>
> *The Patience of Maigret*

- Place 2 cups of flour in a bowl. Make a little hollow in the flour
  and in this put 1 beaten egg, ½ cup of sugar, and a package of
  vanilla sugar (or ½ tsp. of vanilla extract—Tr.). Mix with a fork.
- Little by little, add ½ cup of softened butter. Using the hands,
  mix rapidly until all the flour is absorbed.
- Smooth the dough with the palm of the hand, then form it into a
  ball. Put in a cool place for 2 hours.
- Place 3 eggs in a saucepan and beat with 9 Tb. of sugar. Add
  ¼ cup of finely ground almonds, a dash of cinnamon, and ⅔ cup
  of flour. Beat with a wire whisk.
- Bring 2 cups of milk to a boil and pour over the egg mixture.
  Again beat with a wire whisk. Place on a low flame and cook until
  thick, stirring constantly. Remove from fire and cool.
- Roll out the dough to a thickness of ¼-inch and place in a 9-inch
  French-style tart pan (see Note, page 137, for a description of
  this—Tr.). Pour in the cooled custard.
- Wash, dry, and pit about 1 lb. of *mirabelles* (any small plum
  may be substituted for the *mirabelles*—Tr.).
- Arrange fruits on custard and bake in a moderate oven about
  35 minutes.
- With a little butter, some water and sugar, make a caramel syrup
  (cook until it separates into hard threads when dropped into cold
  water—Tr.). Sprinkle the warm syrup with cinnamon. When it is
  hard, crush it by pounding. Sprinkle over the tart as soon as it
  comes out of the oven. Cool the tart before serving.

COURTINE'S NOTE: When the edges of the tart are a golden brown,
you can cover it with a piece of aluminum foil. This prevents burning.

With the *tarte aux prunes*, Maigret drank *Perrier-Jouët, cuvée
Belle Époque*.

Tarte au Riz

(Rice Tart)

> "I've come to pay my respects. Would you by any chance
> have some of that delicious *tarte au riz?*"
>
> *The Flemish Shop*

- Make a *pâte brisée* according to recipe on page 138. Form dough into a ball, wrap in wax paper, and keep in a cool place for several hours.
- Roll out the dough and place it in a buttered French-style tart pan (See Note, page 137, for a description of this—Tr.). Prick the dough with a fork.
- Wash ¾ cup of rice carefully, place it in 4 qts. of boiling water, and boil for 5 minutes. Drain.
- Put the drained rice into 4 cups of boiling milk to which a vanilla bean has been added. Cook the rice very slowly, without stirring, for ½ hour. Add ½ cup of sugar and cook for 15 minutes.
- Remove the vanilla bean. Add ½ cup of currants, which have been soaked in white rum, together with ½ cup of chopped candied fruits to the cooked rice and place in the pastry shell. Bake in a hot oven (400°) for 15 minutes. Sprinkle with sugar, cool, and serve.

COURTINE'S NOTE: If you use non-pasteurized milk in this recipe, it will improve the result.

With the *tarte au riz*, Maigret drank a small glass of *Genièvre*. (This is a common "local drink" in many parts of northern France. It is similar to Holland gin.   Tr.)

Tarte aux Amandes

(*Almond Tart*)

> "I'm writing to Jaquette to ask her for the recipe for
> the *tarte aux amandes* you're so fond of."
>
> *Maigret in Society*

- Make a *pâte brisée* as in recipe on page 138.
- Roll out the dough and place it in a buttered French-style tart pan (see Note, page 137, for a description of this—Tr.).
- Mix 1 cup of finely chopped, toasted almonds with 2½ cups of powdered sugar, 2 cups of heavy cream,* and 1 Tb. of liqueur.
- Pour the mixture into the uncooked pastry shell and bake for 25 minutes in a hot oven. Serve warm.

COURTINE'S NOTE: You can use any liqueur you happen to be partial to. Madame Maigret is sometimes tempted by *Noyau de Poissy*.

With the *tarte aux amandes*, Maigret drank *Château d'Yquem*.

* This is French *crème fraîche*, much thicker than ordinary heavy cream. Consult Note, p. 129.

Crêpes Suzette

> He took him to Les Halles and ordered *tripes à la mode de Caen* and *crêpes Suzette* that were served in a pretty copper chafing dish.
>
> *The Methods of Maigret*

- Sift 4 Tb. of sugar, 1¼ cups of flour, and a pinch of salt into a bowl.
- Make a hollow in the center and break an egg into it. Stir with a wooden spoon. Stirring all the time, add another egg, then another egg (3 eggs in all). Add little by little 1 cup of slightly cooled boiled milk, beating with a wire whisk until the mixture is smooth. Let stand for 1 hour.
- Add 2 tsp. of Curaçao and 2 tsp. of tangerine juice. Make the *crêpes*. (See Courtine's Note below—Tr.)
- Rub 2 lumps of sugar on the rind of 2 tangerines. Place 4 Tb. of softened butter in a bowl with 3 Tb. of sugar. Cream with a wooden spoon. Add the sugar lumps that have been impregnated with the tangerine rind, the juice of 2 tangerines, and 2 tsp. of Curaçao. Continue to stir until the mixture is soft and completely blended. Place 1 tsp. of this fragrant butter on top of each crêpe while it is very hot. Fold the crêpe in four. Pile the crêpes on a hot platter and serve.

COURTINE'S NOTE: Make the crêpes one by one in a small heavy-bottomed skillet. Pour into it a little clarified butter, heat, then pour a ladleful of crêpe batter (the ladle should hold from 2 to 3 Tb. of batter; test for size yourself—Tr.). When the crêpe is a light brown, turn it and cook the other side. Slide the cooked crêpe onto a very hot plate. Repeat operation until all the crêpes are cooked.

With the *crêpes Suzette*, Maigret drank *Cuvée Florens-Louis* (*Piper Heidsieck*).

Gâteau aux Fraises

(*Wild Strawberry Cake*)

> They savored their *ris de veau* which were delicious.
> Then they had tiny chops, and for dessert a
> *gâteau aux fraises.*
>
> *Maigret and the Madwoman*

- Beat ¾ cup of sugar with 3 eggs.
- Slowly add 2 cups of flour, 2 tsp. of baking powder, and 1 Tb. of water. Mix well.
- Wash ¾ lb. of wild strawberries in water to which a tiny bit of vinegar has been added. Drain and place on a paper towel to dry.
- Powder the wild strawberries with flour and shake them. Add to the cake dough along with 1 tsp. of strawberry liqueur.
- Pour into a buttered cake pan and bake in a moderate oven for 40 minutes.
- Cool the cake, unmold, and serve with whipped cream.

COURTINE'S NOTE: When whipping cream, remember to start beating slowly and increase the speed as you beat.

With the *gâteau aux fraises*, Maigret drank *Champagne Pol Roger rosé*.

Gâteau Moka

(*Cake with Coffee-cream Filling*)

> *Cèpes à la bordelaise* . . . *coq au vin* . . . *gâteau moka*
> . . . *Beaujolais* . . . old *armagnac* . . .
>
> "Have you enjoyed your meal, Monsieur Maigret?" asked
> the truculent Mélanie, who stood higher than any
> celebrity in the eyes of her patrons, and who treated
> everybody with a maternal familiarity. "I once gave you
> the cake recipe for Madame Maigret. Has she ever
> tried it?"
>
> *Cécile est morte*

- Using a wooden spoon, mix 8 egg yolks with 3 cups of powdered sugar. Beat 8 egg whites until stiff and add to yolks along with 1 cup of cornstarch. Flavor with 1 tsp. of lemon juice.
- Place this mixture in a (fairly small, say, 6–8-inch) round buttered cake pan.
- Bake 1 hour in a slow oven. Cool.
- Remove cake from pan. Cut into ¾-inch layers.
- Beat 4 egg whites until stiff. Mix with 2½ cups of powdered sugar. Place in a saucepan over a very low fire and stir until completely blended.
- Remove saucepan from fire and add about 3 tsp. of very strong coffee (taste before adding more.—Tr.). Little by little beat in 1 cup of softened sweet butter.
- Spread the *crème moka* on each layer of cake. Re-form the cake by placing the layers on top of each other. Spread the rest of the *crème moka* on top of the cake.

COURTINE'S NOTE: A few drops of brandy or *crème de cacao* may be added to the *crème moka*.

With the *gâteau moka*, Maigret drank *Dom Pérignon*.

Profiteroles au Chocolat

For dessert Rose brought in an enormous platter of *profiteroles*. The old lady watched Maigret out of her mischievous eyes.

Maigret Afraid

- Place 2 cups of water, 1 cup minus 2 Tb. of butter, 4 tsp. of sugar, and a pinch of salt in a saucepan. Bring to a boil. Cook a few seconds, then remove from fire.
- Pour 2½ cups of flour all at once into the hot liquid, stirring briskly with a wooden spatula.
- Place the saucepan on a very low fire in order to dry out the dough. Stir continuously with a wooden spatula. When the dough no longer clings to the sides of the pan or the spatula, remove pan from fire.
- Add one beaten egg, mixing vigorously and for a long time. Then add, one by one, beating after each addition, 3 more beaten eggs. Stir until eggs are completely absorbed by the dough.
- Butter a baking sheet and place teaspoonfuls of the dough on it, allowing plenty of room for expansion. Brush each one with a little beaten egg yolk. Place in a preheated moderate oven.
- Bake for about 25 minutes (until puffed). The puffs should not be allowed to get too brown as this will dry them out.
- Remove puffs from baking sheet. Cool.
- Place ⅔ cup of water, ½ cup of unsweetened cocoa, and 1 cup of sugar in a saucepan. Bring to a boil. Simmer, stirring with a wooden spoon, for about 10 minutes, until a smooth sauce has formed.
- Mix 2 tsp. of potato flour (or cornstarch) with a little cold water. Add to the hot chocolate mixture. Place on a very low flame and stir until thick. Remove from fire and keep warm over hot water.
- For each serving, place 4 or 5 puffs in a crystal dessert dish. Garnish with vanilla ice cream. Over all, pour the chocolate sauce reheated until boiling hot.

COURTINE'S NOTE: People with a real sweet tooth replace the cocoa with sweetened chocolate, but true connoisseurs realize that the pleasure of *profiteroles* lies in a marriage of opposites: cold, sweet ice cream and hot, bitter sauce.

With the *profiteroles*, Maigret drank *Blason de France* (*Perrier-Jouët*).

Baba au Rhum

> They ate *rillettes du pays*, *coq au vin blanc*, and, after
> the goat cheese, *babas au rhum*.
>
> *Maigret and the Killer*

- Dissolve a yeast cake (or one pkg. of dry yeast) in 2 Tb. of luke-warm milk.
- Mix with ⅔ cup of flour. Knead until smooth and elastic. Let rise in a warm place for 7 hours in a covered bowl.
- Place the raised dough in a large bowl and add ½ cup of butter, a pinch of salt, 2 cups of flour, 3 eggs, and 1 cup of confectionery sugar. Knead vigorously for 10 minutes.
- Add ½ cup of currants that have been soaked in dark rum and drained.
- Thickly butter a ring mold, and place the dough in it. (The mold should be half full.) Bake in a slow oven for 50 minutes.
- Place the baba on a platter and drench it (while it is still fairly hot) with rum sauce.

COURTINE'S NOTE: To make the rum sauce, heat ⅔ cup of sugar with 2 cups of water. When it boils, add 1 cup of rum. Bring to a boil again and remove from heat.

With the *baba au rhum*, Maigret drank *Champagne Pol Roger* 1966.

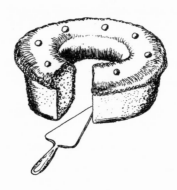

Gâteau de Riz à la Normande

(*Rice Tart Normandy Style*)

> The maid had just set a *gâteau de riz* in the middle of the round table, and Maigret had to make an effort to appear at once surprised and blissfully happy. Madame Pardon blushed and gave him a mischievous glance.
>
> *Maigret Has Doubts*

- Boil 4 cups of milk with a vanilla bean and a pinch of salt.
- Pour ½ cup of rice into the milk and stir with a wooden spatula until it boils again. Cover and place in a moderate oven for 35 minutes. (Remove vanilla bean before putting in oven.)
- Remove from oven and cool slightly. Add 4 Tb. of sugar. Mix a little boiled milk with 4 egg yolks and add to milk and rice mixture along with 2 Tb. of butter cut in pieces. Mix carefully with a fork so as not to break the grains of rice.
- Peel 5 large tart apples. Cut them in quarters and scoop out the cores. Cook them slowly in butter. While they are cooking, sprinkle them with sugar and grated lemon peel.
- With a fork mash half the cooked apples. Bind them together with 2 Tb. of hot cream and mix with the rice.
- Coat a pudding mold with caramel. (To do this, sprinkle the mold with sugar and heat it in a slow oven until the sugar is brown—Tr.) On the bottom of the mold place the remaining apple quarters. Add the rice mixture. (The mold should not be over ¾ full.)
- Cover with buttered wax paper and bake in a moderate oven for 40 minutes.
- Cool and unmold.

COURTINE'S NOTE: This dessert may be served with custard sauce or syrup. A syrup made of fresh currants or raspberries with a dash of Calvados is excellent.

With the *gâteau de riz*, Maigret drank *Saint-Péray*.

Oeufs au Lait

(Egg Custard)

Maigret was eating his dessert when he became conscious
of the way his wife was looking at him, with a slightly
mocking and maternal smile. He pretended not to notice,
went back to his dessert, and took a few more bites of
his *oeufs au lait* before raising his eyes.

Maigret and the Headless Corpse

- Boil 4 cups of milk with a vanilla bean and ¾ cup of sugar.
- Beat 4 eggs.
- Mix with the milk, stirring with a wooden spoon. Remove the
  vanilla bean and pour the egg and milk mixture into an ovenproof
  dish, or custard cups.
- Bake 45 minutes in a slow oven.

COURTINE'S NOTE: For flavoring you might replace the vanilla bean
with orange-flower water, rum, or anisette.

With the *oeufs au lait*, Maigret drank *Muscat*.

Crème au Citron

(*Lemon Custard*)

> "I've got an idea! I'll make you a *crème au citron*.
> . . . I hope they'll let me use the kitchen. . . ."
>
> *The Madman of Bergerac*

- Boil 4 cups of milk with 2 tsp. of lemon extract and ½ cup of sugar.
- Beat 6 egg yolks. Add them to the milk, beating constantly.
- Cook in a double boiler, watching that the custard does not boil. When it has thickened, remove from fire and strain. Cool and serve.

COURTINE'S NOTE: You can add 1 tsp. of kirsch just before straining the custard.

With the *crème au citron*, Maigret drank ice water.

Crème au Caramel

(*Caramel Custard*)

> And tomorrow, since he had the grippe, Madame Maigret
> would make him a *crème au caramel.*
>
> *Le Témoignage de l'Enfant de Choeur*

- Make a caramel sauce by mixing and cooking ¾ cup of sugar and
  1 Tb. of butter. When it is dark brown, lower heat and slowly add
  3 tsp. of water, stirring until blended.
- Pour this liquid into 4 cups of hot milk.
- Put 6 egg yolks in a saucepan and mix in 6 Tb. of sugar.
- Add the hot milk and caramel mixture to the egg yolks very slowly,
  stirring constantly. Place the saucepan over a low fire.
- Stir and cook until the custard thickens and coats the spoon.

COURTINE'S NOTE: If, in the process of cooking, the custard separates,
bind it together by beating it with an egg beater.

With the *crème au caramel*, Maigret drank *Frontignan*.

Crème au Chocolat

(*Chocolate Custard*)

"I don't know . . . I was busy making the *crème*. . . ."
L'Amoureux de Madame Maigret

- Melt 3 squares of semi-sweet chocolate in ½ cup of hot water.
- When the chocolate is completely dissolved, add 2 cups of milk and bring to a boil. Turn off heat.
- In a bowl mix 5 egg yolks with ½ cup of sugar. Add little by little to the chocolate mixture. Place on a low flame, stirring, until it thickens.
- Remove saucepan from fire. Add 4 stiffly beaten egg whites. Place over heat for an instant, stirring. As soon as the mixture approaches boiling, remove from fire and pour it in a bowl.

COURTINE'S NOTE: To change the flavor, add a bit of cinnamon to the chocolate and water mixture. Or a teaspoon of brandy, rum, armagnac, Scotch whisky, etc.

With the *crème au chocolat*, Maigret drank ice water.

Wine Glossary

Wine Glossary

by Jack Lang

Aligoté

This white Burgundy can be found here, but unless dirt cheap, it's not worth it. Better to find a reputable merchant selling a tested Pinot Chardonnay, Blanc de Blancs, or treat yourself to one of the whole gamut of superior white Burgundies: Pouilly-Fuissé, Corton-Charlemagne, Chablis, Château du Vire (the best of the Mâcon Blancs), or a dry white Graves.

Beaujolais Primeur

Primeur is a ninety-day wonder, for that is the time it spends barreled. It is brash, fruity, and *gouleyant* (meaning "one glass leads to another"). The best is enjoyed in France; the rest travels not too spectacularly. Instead, perhaps, one should look for a good Beaujolais-Villages, Brouilly, Fleurie, one of the village wines of the Côte de Nuits or the Côte de Beaune, or the early maturing wines of the southernmost part of the Côte d'Or, such as Rully, Mercurey, or Givry. An American substitute might be a (California) Gamay Beaujolais, Zinfandel, or Burgundy.

Beaujolais-Villages

Available here from coast to coast, but with popularity should go caution. Any *real* Beaujolais can be used. As for U.S.A. (California), try Zinfandel, or any young, brash, fruity red like Ruby Cabernet, Gamay, Gamay Beaujolais, Barbera, or Grignolino.

Blanc de l'Île de Ré

Île de Ré is off the southwest coast of France, approximately opposite the area of Cognac. The island's seacoast is awash with the seaweed used to fertilize the vineyards. The resultant wine has a unique smoky (*fumé*) quality. There is a degree of interest by importers here to bring this wine to us, but till that happens, focus on the Loire

Valley's Pouilly-Fumés, Sancerres, or Quincys; or take a Traminer or a Gewürztraminer from the Alsace; or try a Fumé Blanc or a Chenin Blanc from California.

Blanc de Ménetou-Salon

The wine originates from near Bourges, in the middle of France, and is made from the Sauvignon Blanc grape. The same grape, grown in Bordeaux, produces the great white Graves; in the Loire Valley, where it is known as Blanc-Fumé, it gives the charm, fruit, and fleeting qualities of Pouilly-Fumé, Sancerre, and Quincy. On our own West Coast (California), the grape gives slightly less taut wines, such as Fumé Blanc and Sauvignon Blanc.

Blason de France (Perrier-Jouët)

See CHAMPAGNE.

Bordeaux Côtes de Fronsac

The wines of Fronsac are full-bodied, with good fruit. They resemble the Saint-Émilions but are less distinguished. The best châteaux are Château Canon and Château La Dauphine, but when purchasing, it might be simpler to ask for the *appellation* "Côtes de Fronsac," rather than for a particular château, for distribution is limited here. Easier to find will be the wines of the Côtes de Bourg, and, of course, Saint-Émilion. Spanish Claretes will do, as well as the Cabernet Sauvignons and Clarets of California. From New York, look for the light reds of the Bully Hill, High Tor, and Boordy vineyards. If you see the New York State red labeled Chelois, try it.

Bourgueil

Bourgueil and Chinon are the best reds from Touraine in the Loire Valley. At optimum when young (*de l'année*, meaning "of the, or this, year"), served fairly cool, their fruit, freshness, delicacy, and charm emerge. They may not be the easiest wines to find, and if found, might be past their youth and not worth drinking. Instead, then, look for a young Beaujolais-Villages, a Corbières or Minervois (both young reds from the Midi), or a good Chalonnaise red like Givry, Rully, and

Mercurey. From New York State, try Baco Noir or Lake Country Red; and from California, Zinfandel, Gamay, Gamay Beaujolais, or any of the mountain reds.

Cahors

Cahors is known as the black wine of France, so deep is its color. It is also very full-bodied, firmly textured, extremely long-lived, and slow to mature. It should be aerated for a longer time than most reds before drinking. There is a definite affinity between Cahors and the full, generous reds of the Italian Piedmont like Ghemme, Gattinara, Barolo, and Sassella. The red Bordeaux of St. Estèphe, Pauillac, and Graves will be noble replacements. A red Hermitage or Côte Rôtie, both famous for power and authority, will also do well. From California, first the Cabernet Sauvignons, then the Pinot Noirs; nothing from New York can fill in here.

Chambolle-Musigny

The village is Chambolle, the finest vineyard, Musigny. Typical of many other Burgundian villages, it has added the name of its best vineyard to the town name and is now called Chambolle-Musigny. The wines here are delicate, charming, and among the most fragrant. The best is labeled "Musigny," leaving off "Chambolle," and the next best always carry vineyard names after Chambolle-Musigny, such as "Les Charmes," or "Les Amoureuses." Locating these wines will not be difficult, though paying for them might, so consider also the regionals by reputable shippers, or a Moulin-à-Vent, or a Morgon (these two are the fullest-bodied *Grands Crus* of Beaujolais and most closely resemble Burgundies). You could try the great Chilean wine called Casiliero del Diablo, or some of the well-seasoned Reservas from Spain that come in Burgundy-shaped bottles. From California, Pinot Noir, Red Pinot, Burgundy, and Petite-Sirah.

Champagne

Only the sparkling wines made from grapes grown in the French province of Champagne are rightfully called Champagne, for they are unique. Champagne can be served with practically everything, and should come to the glass only from an ice-bucket. (The greatest champagne, not cold enough, can be cloying.) Maigret's choice of champagnes includes the premier products of the great producers. Here, their cost would be high. When price is a factor in choice, look for store specials and unadvertised brands. California and New York State are both producers of sparkling wine labeled "Champagne." So select and taste, and then select again.

Châteaugay

Produced from the Gamay grape, grown in practically solid chalk, Châteaugay is not available here. The charming wines of Beaujolais and the Mâcon bear the closest resemblance. Various Mâcon Rouges (and Blancs) are ubiquitous: they are dry, pleasant, have a touch of "the taste of the earth" (*goût de terroir*), and should be had young. Any reliable Beaujolais will substitute. From California, try Gamay, Gamay Beaujolais, and Burgundy. From New York, look for Baco Noir, Bully Hill Red, High Tor Red, or Rubicon.

Château Giscours (Margaux)

Among the wines of the Haut-Médoc, those of Margaux are unique for their great finesse, delicacy, and unbelievable bouquet. Château Giscours, once almost in disrepute, is now one of the great clarets of Margaux. It should not be hard to find, but any of the classified châteaux of Margaux will offer similar pleasure. For present use, look for the 1967's, 64's, 62's. For laying away, 1966, 1970, 1971. The Cabernet Sauvignons of California have not achieved the intriguing complexities of a Margaux, so if you're shopping American, buy only the best.

Château Lacoste (Côteaux d'Aix)

This red wine of Provence is not available here. Look, instead, for a good *petit château, Cru Bourgeois*, young red Bordeaux vinified for early maturity and consumption, or a reputable, also young, Côtes du Rhône, Corbières, or Minervois. Any number of red jug wines will also do; try a red of the Côtes de Bourg, generally well balanced and reasonable in price. In America we have dry dry reds labeled as Clarets that can be had cold (if a wine is not very good, drink it cold, drink it fast!), or we can go to their truer selves and select one labeled Cabernet Sauvignon.

Château Léoville-Las-Cases

An absolutely great red from Saint-Julien in the Haut-Médoc. Like
all good Saint-Juliens, the wine is "out of balance," delightfully so,
in the direction of fruit. Alternates are a Ducru-Beaucaillou, Léoville-
Poyferré, Gruaud-Larose, Beychevelle, or a Talbot. From South
America, Chilean Cabernet and Casiliero del Diablo; from Yugoslavia,
Cabernet and Plavac; and from Spain, the best of Rioja's Clarete
Reservas. In this country, the California Cabernet Sauvignons, Petite-
Sirahs, and Zinfandels. From New York State, Chelois, Baco Noir,
Bully Hill Red, Boordy Cabernet Sauvignon.

Château Magence (Graves Blanc)

Consult GRAVES.

Châteauneuf-du-Pape

One of the three great red wines of the Rhône Valley: exceptionally
generous, robust, full-bodied. The best are estate-bottled and,
depending on the nature of the vintage, should be five to nine years
old. Côte Rôtie and Hermitage, the other two great reds, should be
a little older. Younger Rhônes worth using are Gigondas, Chusclan,
and Côtes du Ventoux. An unbelievably great wine from California is
a Petite-Sirah from Ridge Vineyard—worth searching for! Try,
too, other California Petite-Sirahs, Pinot Noirs, or Cabernet
Sauvignons. New York State has nothing like this.

Château Pétrus

See POMEROL.

Château Poujeaux (Moulis-Médoc)

A light red Bordeaux of the Haut-Médoc from the *commune* of Moulis.
Château Poujeaux does come here, but Château Chasse-Spleen, the
best of the Moulis, is easier to find and is relatively reasonable. From
outside Moulis but still in the Haut-Médoc are the excellent wines of
Château de Camensac and Château Cissac—actually any of the
reputable châteaux of Bordeaux, both classified and *Cru Bourgeois*, will
provide pleasurable alternatives. Other considerations: a Yugoslav

Cabernet or a Plavac, a Rioja from Spain labeled Clarete, or a
Californian Cabernet Sauvignon.

Château de Selle Rouge

Château de Selle is available here in rosé and white, but not red. A
good Beaujolais, especially Fleurie, will do equally well.

Château d'Yquem

This, the only *Premier Grand Cru* (first great growth) of Sauternes,
is the quintessence of lusciousness. Honey-colored and rich, expensive
and rare, it is revered by wine-lovers the world over. There are other
wonderful Sauternes—look for them and enjoy them—but there is
nothing like Château d'Yquem. Serve it at about 58°—never ice-cold.

Chianti

Look for Chianti labeled "*classico*"; the best Chiantis are always
classico, and come in Bordeaux-shaped bottles. Their vintage dates are
authentic, and if you come across a great one, it's really a "kissing
cousin" to a good Bordeaux. Lighter and more delicate are the
well-known Valpolicella and Bardolino wines. From California try
Barbera, Grignolino, and Charbono.

Chinon

Maigret probably drank a Chinon red, though this little town of the
Loire Valley produces whites and rosés as well. Please look at
comments under BOURGUEIL.

Chiroubles

Another great and favorite Beaujolais. See the comments about
FLEURIE.

Cider

French cider is *hard* cider and it is possible to find in wineshops, or
in gourmet grocery stores. If necessary, you can substitute a demi-sec
(half-dry) Vouvray, or an Alsatian Riesling. Or try one of the many

apple wines now available from different parts of the U.S.A.—some
are apple-flavored grape wines, but there is a true apple wine from
Vermont that is dry yet not acidic, with a tautness and taste truly
characteristic of the fruit.

Corent

Same situation as with Châteaugay—not available. See suggestions
under that heading.

Cornas

Cornas and Saint-Joseph are good, sturdy, dry red wines of the
Rhône Valley. These can be found, but may take some looking. Easier
to find are Côtes du Rhône, Gigondas, Côtes du Ventoux—all Rhône
reds. From California, look for Petite-Sirah, Zinfandel, or Barbera.

Corton Blanc

One cannot tell what Corton Blanc 1967 the inspector had, but
here, if we drink a Corton Blanc, it will probably be Corton-
Charlemagne, one of the greatest of all the white Burgundies—subtle
but authoritative, dry, but also giving fruit and bouquet. For alternate
suggestions, see comments on RULLY.

Corton-Grancey

Corton-Grancey is red, one of the great Cortons, and is available here.
Bottled at Château Grancey in Aloxe-Corton, this wine is soft,
well-fruited, full-bodied, and with big bouquet. There is also Corton-
Clos du Roi, Corton-Bressandes, and village wine labeled Aloxe-
Corton. Easy to find and worth looking for are Volnay and Monthélie,
the latter little known and worthy of greater recognition. From
California: Pinot Noir, Petite-Sirah, and Burgundy. New York State
has Baco Noir and Chelois.

Costières-du-Gard

A wine from southwestern France, where quantity supersedes quality
and most of the *vin ordinaire* comes from. We get other better wines
here from the same region. The closest to Maigret's choice are

Corbières and Minervois; they are usually carafe wines in France. Consider, instead, a red wine from some of the smaller but excellent châteaux of Bordeaux; available, reasonable, and appropriate. From Hungary try their best red, called Egri Bikavér, or use one of the good Spanish reds of Rioja. From California, select a Claret or a Cabernet Sauvignon.

Domaine de Chevalier (Graves Blanc *and* Rouge)

See GRAVES.

Domaine des Clairettes (Rosé de Provence)

This light, dry pink wine from the Riviera should be had fresh, young, and slightly chilled. It should be easy to locate, but any of the California Gamay or Grenache Rosés will do just as well. If one desires a fruitier rosé, try those of New York State.

Domaine des Hautes Cornières

See comments on SANTENAY.

Dom Pérignon

See CHAMPAGNE.

Fendant

Available as Fendant de Sion, or du Valais, a delicious wine, very fresh and fine. Good wineshops should have it or be able to order it: don't look for specific vintage years but have it as young as possible. Alternates might be a German Rhine wine—Schloss Johannisberger, Schloss Vollrads, Steinberger—or an Alsatian Riesling or Traminer. From California, select Johannisberg Riesling, Grey Riesling, Chenin Blanc, or dry Sémillon. From New York State, Dr. Konstantin Frank's Johannisberg Riesling.

Fleurie

One of the greatest wines of the Beaujolais and, perhaps, the most typical—it gives all the fragrance, balance, and charm one could

possibly want. Make a special effort to acquire it. If, however, your
search proves fruitless, look for other greats of Beaujolais:
Saint-Amour, Chénas, Chiroubles, Brouilly, Juliénas, Morgon,
Côte de Brouilly, or the noble Moulin-à-Vent. The Gamay
Beaujolais from California is excellent, but it just isn't Fleurie.

Frontignan

See MUSCAT DE FRONTIGNAN.

Genièvre

This is not a gin for martinis. It comes in a crock, should be served
from the freezer (don't worry, it won't freeze), and taken neat.
The brand easiest to find and probably the best, is Bols
Genever Gin.

Graves (Blanc *and* Rouge)

The Graves district of Bordeaux produces red and white wines—
the reds vigorous and full-bodied, the whites dry, crisp, racy, with
a subtle hint of almonds in the aftertaste. There is no argument,
generally, about Château Haut-Brion being the greatest red of Graves,
and there are some experts who consider it top among the whites.
Maigret appears to prefer the wines, both white and red, of Domaine
de Chevalier, and his choice won't be difficult to find here. Look, as
well, for Château La Mission-Haut-Brion, or Château Pape-Clément
if you desire a red Graves, or substitute any of the classified châteaux
of Bordeaux. For white Graves, consider the great wines of Châteaux
Carbonnieux, Olivier, Bouscaut, or Laville-Haut-Brion. Smaller
châteaux producing beautifully typical Graves are: La Louvière and
Domaine des Plantes. From California, you may, if necessary,
substitute for red Graves a Cabernet Sauvignon, but choose only the
best: from New York State, possibly a High Tor Red, a Bully Hill Red,
a Boordy Cabernet Sauvignon, or a Chelois. For a white, try a
California Sauvignon Blanc or dry Sémillon.

Gris de Toul

See VIN GRIS DE TOUL.

Gros Plant Nantais

This light, refreshing, dry white wine from Nantes in the Loire Valley is probably not on the shelves of your wineshop. Try looking for Muscadet sur lie or Sancerre. From California, a Folle Blanche, Chablis, Emerald Dry Riesling, or Pinot Blanc. From New York State, try to find Chablis Nature, Bully Hill White, and Seyval Blanc.

Haut-Brion Blanc

See GRAVES.

Hermitage Blanc

A Rhône Valley white, this is a robust, dry, pale-gold wine. Unless properly bottle-aged, it may be harsh, so bypass it in infancy. Available here but in better shops only, the best Hermitage Blanc is labeled Chante-Alouette. The great white Burgundies like Meursault, Corton-Charlemagne, the Montrachets, and Musigny Blanc will give a similar power and authority. Little in American viniculture can match these except, perhaps, a few of the most esoteric California Pinot Chardonnays.

Hermitage Rouge

An aged Hermitage red is likely to be expensive: you might get a young one and keep it in your cellar. The finest Hermitage reds are produced from such vineyards as L'Hermitage, Les Bessards, and Le Méal. For alternates, see comments on CHÂTEAUNEUF-DU-PAPE.

Madiran

This sturdy red wine from southwestern France is not available here. See suggestions for CAHORS, CHÂTEAUNEUF-DU-PAPE, and POMEROL.

Moselle

See RIESLING.

Moulin-à-Vent

The fullest-bodied, longest-lived of all the *Grands Crus* of Beaujolais and closest in resemblance to Burgundy, Moulin-à-Vent is deep crimson in color, with a hint of raspberry in the aftertaste. Not difficult to find, but not inexpensive. See comments on SAINT-AMOUR.

Mumm Cuvée René Lalou

See CHAMPAGNE.

Muscadet de Sèvres-et-Maine tiré sur lie

Muscadet, yes, but do make sure it is young and says "*sur lie*." The wine produced this way is more delicate, flavorful, and also longer-lived. Any of the other Loire Valley whites such as Sancerre, Pouilly-Fumé, Vouvray, and Quincy are also in harmony. Or, from California, choose Fumé Blanc, Chenin Blanc, Pinot Blanc, or a dry Sémillon.

Muscat de Frontignan

From Frontignan on the Mediterranean, made from the Muscat grape, this sweet, fortified (brandy added) dessert wine may be hard to find. Instead, try a good tawny Port, an Amontillado Sherry, or a dry Madeira (Rainwater or Sercial). There are also California Muscats and Malvasias or a New York State Muscat Ottonel by Dr. K. Frank.

Perrier-Jouët, Cuvée Belle Époque

See CHAMPAGNE.

Pinot Rouge

Maigret most likely drank a rosé made from the Pinot Noir grape. Not too easy to find here, but possible. The wine is quite delicious when young and is light, dry, and fruity. Similar will be a Swiss Dôle, but it is ruby, not rosé. From California, try any of the Grenache or Gamay Rosés, or a Grey Riesling, a Traminer, or

167

Gewürztraminer. From New York State, an Aurora Blanc, a
Seyval Blanc, or any of the Lake Country rosés.

Pomerol

The Pomerol district of Bordeaux produces a distinctive velvety red
wine. The single greatest wine of the Pomerol is Château Pétrus—
the softest and most fragrant, with justly famous grace, charm,
fruit. Among other vineyards maintaining the renowned Pomerol
traits are: Châteaux L'Evangile, Gazin, La Conseillante, Lafleur-
Pétrus, Petit-Village, Nénin, Trotanoy, and Vieux-Château-Certan.
There are also very fine smaller châteaux whose wines are
available here.

Pouilly-Chasselas

We will not find this fresh agreeable white wine here under this
name, but rather labeled as Pouilly-sur-Loire. Better to drink and
easier to find will be Pouilly-Fumé, also called Pouilly-Blanc-
Fumé. Drink the wine in its youth to enjoy its racy, dry, yet
fruity taste. One can also look for California approximations,
such as Sauvignon Blanc, Fumé Blanc, or Chenin Blanc.

Pouilly-Fumé

See POUILLY-CHASSELAS.

Prunelle

Several recipes mention Prunelle, a name that can refer to a liqueur
made of the sloe, or brandy made of prunes or flavored by prunes.
For cooking, one would use the brandy. In the U.S.A., you can
purchase prune brandy from France (it could be Alsatian) called
Mirabelle. There is also plum brandy from Israel, Yugoslavia, and
Czechoslovakia called Slivovitz.

Puligny-Montrachet

The villages of Puligny and Chassagne-Montrachet can be said to
produce the finest dry white wines of France—rich, robust, and
fantastically rewarding. Expect to find a generous selection in your

wineshop. Look for the 69's, 70's, 71's, with intent to hold the 71's for a few more years. The wines of these villages are of such great class and breed that it is almost impertinent to suggest alternatives. If one must substitute, consider one of the excellent Pinot Chardonnays from California, or one of Dr. K. Frank's from New York.

Quincy

Most wineshops will not have Quincy, an interesting dry white wine of the Loire Valley. Look instead for Sancerre, Pouilly-Fumé or a Muscadet sur lie. More readily available, from California, would be a Sauvignon Blanc, Chenin Blanc, Pineau de la Loire, or a Fumé Blanc. From New York State, look for Seyval Blanc, Bully Hill White, and Chablis Nature.

Riesling

Practically all of the finest Rhine and Moselle wines are of the Riesling—one of the great white wine grapes of the world—as well as excellent wines of the Alsace, the Italian Tyrol, Austria, Chile, California, and New York. Your choice is wide. Look for good estates of the Mosel-Saar-Ruwer, in at least Cabinet-quality wines; or try a Rheingau, Rheinhessen, or Rheinpfalz, all of Germany. Alsatian Riesling is labeled exactly that way. California has a host of Johannisberg Rieslings, Grey Rieslings, and Emerald Rieslings, but a New York State one can only be of Dr. K. Frank.

Rouge de Bellet

This, coming from Nice on the Riviera, where its youth, charm, and freshness make it attractive, isn't quite as good here. Try instead one of the rosés of Provence, or good, young, brash Beaujolais. There is also excellent jug wine from the Côteaux du Languedoc (distributed here under the name George Bonfils). Zinfandel and Gamay Beaujolais are the best California choices; and Chelois, Baco Noir, Bully Hill Red, and Rubicon from New York State.

Rouge de l'Île de Ré

As mentioned in the comments for Blanc de l'Île de Ré, this wine is not available here. However, the light reds of the Loire, such as

Chinon and Bourgueil, will do handsomely. With *gigot à la bretonne*,
a good Beaujolais would be suitable, or one of the lighter reds of
Bordeaux. If shopping American, ask for Zinfandel, Claret,
Gamay Beaujolais, and Barbera from California; Chelois, Baco Noir,
Bully Hill Red, from New York.

Roussillon

See VIN VERT DU ROUSSILLON.

Rully

Rully originates in the southernmost part of the Côte d'Or, known
as the Côte Chalonnaise. Rully can be red or white; with *sole dieppoise*,
Maigret undoubtedly had the Rully Blanc. Made from all Pinot
Chardonnay grape, the wine is refreshing and supple—worth looking
for. If finding it is a task, however, try the other great white
Burgundies like Pouilly-Fuissé, Pouilly Vinzelles, Montagny, any of
the white Montrachets, or, if you can find it, Nuits-Saint-Georges
Blanc. There is a pleasant white Languedoc in jugs called Ugni
Blanc. From California, Chablis, Pinot Chardonnay, and
Pinot Blanc.

Saint-Amour

Saint-Amour is one of the *Grands Crus* of Beaujolais (only nine are
officially classified this way). The wine is soft, round, fruity,
with beautiful garnet color and lovely bouquet. Enjoy it young.
Consider also the wines of Brouilly, Juliénas, Chénas, Chiroubles,
Côte de Brouilly, and Fleurie. Lesser, yet not to be ignored, are
the wines labeled Beaujolais-Villages, or Côtes du Rhône, or
Gigondas, or Côtes du Ventoux—the last three, Rhône Valley reds.
Out of California, look for Gamay or Gamay Beaujolais, and
Zinfandel. From New York State, Baco Noir and Chelois.

Saint-Nicolas-de-Bourgueil

See BOURGUEIL.

Saint-Péray

This sparkling wine from Saint-Péray in the Rhône Valley is amber-colored, full-bodied, less elegant than Champagne, but also much lower-priced and highly enjoyable. Popular in France, probably not available here. We do import, from Seyssell in the Haute-Savoie, an excellent *vin mousseux* known as Le Duc. Lighter and cheaper than Saint-Péray, it is worth finding. American sparkling wines labeled as "Champagne" can also be used.

Saint-Pourçain Blanc

Absolutely unavailable! Try Beaujolais Blanc, or Mâcon Vire, or Pinot Chardonnay. From California, look for Folle Blanche, dry Sémillon, or your favorite champagne.

Saint-Pourçain Rouge

A light, dry red wine, with a mild touch of fruit, produced from the Gamay grape along tributaries of the Loire. Unavailable here. Its best approximations are listed under BOURGUEIL.

Santenay, Domaine des Hautes Cornières

This is available in the U.S.A.—Frank Schoonmaker, a great and reputable importer specializing in Burgundies, has imported it. It is from the southernmost part of the Côte d'Or, where soft, velvety reds of fine texture and bouquet are produced. Also consider a Mercurey, Rully, Givry, Meursault-Blagny, or a Chassagne-Montrachet Rouge: for these, estate-bottling is important, although there are excellent regionals (Charles Ninot, for one). From California, use Pinot Noir, Red Pinot, Pinot St. Georges, or Burgundy. From New York State, Baco Noir or Chelois.

Sylvaner

The most popular Sylvaners are Alsatian, not expensive, and not hard to find. The best (and most esoteric) come in squat bottles, called "bocksbeutels," from Würzburg in Germany and are known as Frankenwein. Look for these first, or try to find a Kremser or

Gumpoldskirchner from Austria; from the Alto Adige in Northern Italy, look for the fresh and lovely light wines of the Tyrol, or from California, Grey Riesling, Johannisberg Riesling, or Emerald Riesling. From New York State, look only for Dr. K. Frank's Johannisberg Riesling.

Tavel

Probably the best, driest, and most characterful French rosé is from Tavel in the Rhône Valley. Buy it when young, serve it fairly chilled. Other excellent rosés are from Provence, Anjou, and from the Côte de Nuits near Dijon where the best is called Rosé de Marsannay. From California, look for Grenache Rosé, Gamay Rosé, Napa Rosé, Vin Rosé Sec, and possibly Zinfandel Rosé and Cabernet Rosé, these last two rather hard to find. From New York State, expect them to be quite fruity, but try Boordy, Bully Hill, or the Lake Country wines from around the Finger Lakes area.

Tokay d'Alsace

The original and true Tokay is Hungarian; the name refers to a district which produces rich and luscious wines, not inexpensive, similar to the great French Sauternes and the German Trockenbeerenauslese. Tokay of the Alsace is produced from a different grape, the Pinot Gris, and is also full-bodied, either dry or slightly sweet. If you can't find what Maigret had, choose a Rhine and Moselle labeled Spätlese or Auslese, or a slightly sweet Rioja from Spain called Brillante. From California, try a dry or sweet Sémillon, or a good vineyard's Johannisberg Riesling. From New York State, try Delaware, Lake Niagara, Diamond, or Seyval Blanc.

Villaudric

An undistinguished red or white wine from the environs of the town named Villaudric and not available here. Instead, use Corton-Grancey, Hermitage Rouge, Cahors, or any vigorous red wine you have had good experience with, imported or American.

Vin Blanc Niçois de Bellet

You will not find it here. Easy to find are many Côtes de Provence whites; among the best are Château de Selle, Château Saint-Roseline, and Domaine du Galoupet. If searching does not turn these up, look for a good Mâcon Blanc, any of the great white Burgundies such as Chablis, Meursault, the Montrachets, or a dry white Graves. From California: Pinot Chardonnay, Grey Riesling, Folle Blanche, or the dry mountain whites. New York State offers Bully Hill White and Boordy Vineyard White.

Vin Gris de Toul

Probably unavailable, this is light dry wine from Toul in the province of Lorraine. Instead, look for one of the agreeable wines of Alsace labeled Sylvaner, Riesling, or Traminer, or use a light, racy white of Graves. California produces Traminer, but easier to find are the Johannisberg Rieslings, Grey Rieslings, and Emerald Rieslings. From New York State, look for Dr. K. Frank's Johannisberg Riesling and Pinot Chardonnay.

Vin de Jasnières

Don't even waste a phone call; you won't find this one. I'm sure Maigret would have also enjoyed Muscadet sur lie, Sancerre, Pouilly-Fumé, or—only from a trusted source—Pinot Chardonnay and Blanc de Blancs. From California, Chenin Blanc, Sauvignon Blanc, or Fumé Blanc. New York State offers Chablis Nature and the fine Pinot Chardonnay of Dr. K. Frank.

Vin Vert du Roussillon

"*Vin vert*" means "green wine," which means "young wine." Maigret drank a young white wine from the French side of the Pyrenees—an area more famous for its volume than its quality. What he had is not to be found here. Instead, we'll fill the glass with appropriate French wines: a good, austere Chablis, or a less austere white of the Côtes de Provence, or a charming Pouilly-Fuissé. Or look for a white called Jurançon, hard to find, but rewarding, and it is inexpensive. One can select—be very careful—a Spanish Vino Blanco from a reputable shipper like Federico Paternina (Hemingway's favorite) or Bodegas Bilbainas or Cune; in larger sizes, half gallons and gallons, look for La Tarra. From Portugal look for Vinho Verde. Of American wines pick a Chablis, Pinot Chardonnay, Sauvignon Blanc, Pinot Blanc, or Chenin Blanc.

Vouvray

A Loire Valley white wine, Vouvray can be sparkling (*pétillant*),
or still. Depending on vintage and vinification, it can be dry and
fruity, acidic and tart, rich and sweet. Sancerre, Pouilly-Fumé, and
Muscadet sur lie are also Loire Valley dry whites, and are good
alternates. An Italian Soave or Frascati, both easy to find, will also be
satisfying. From California, try a Chenin Blanc, a Fumé Blanc,
Pineau Souvrain, or a Pineau de la Loire. From New York State, a
Seyval Blanc, Bully Hill White, High Tor or Boordy Vineyard
Whites, or an Aurora.

Index

Index

S

T